T0157999

IDENTIFICATION:
FRIEND OR FOE

DEATH BY FRIENDLY FIRE,
DISCOVERED SIXTY-TWO YEARS LATER

JAMES MACLEOD M.D.

Order this book online at www.trafford.com
or email orders@trafford.com

Most Trafford titles are also available at major online book retailers.

© Copyright 2012 James MacLeod.
All rights reserved. No part of this publication may be reproduced, stored in a retrieval system,
or transmitted, in any form or by any means, electronic, mechanical, photocopying, recording,
or otherwise, without the written prior permission of the author.

Printed in the United States of America.

ISBN: 978-1-4669-2089-7 (sc)
ISBN: 978-1-4669-2186-3 (e)

Trafford rev. 11/26/2012

 www.trafford.com

North America & international
toll-free: 1 888 232 4444 (USA & Canada)
phone: 250 383 6864 ♦ fax: 812 355 4082

My older brother Dewar and I grew up in Halifax. Nova Scotia. During the Second World War, he entered the Royal Canadian Air Force (RCAF), became a pilot and a Flying Officer. After a year as an instructor, he was attached to the Second Tactical Air Force, flying Mosquito aircraft in support of Allied ground forces in Europe.

When I came of age (17), I too enrolled in the RCAF and became a bomb-aimer (bombardier). When I arrived in England, I visited him and flew with him in his "Mosquito".

Ten days later, September 29, 1944, my brother was killed in action. That was all I knew, for sixty-two years, until July 26, 2006, when a notice appeared in the Halifax newspaper.

The ChronicleHerald.ca

» The NovaScotian

HALIFAX, NOVA SCOTIA | Tuesday July 18, 2006

2006-07-15, Letters
LOST AND FOUND
Clan MacLeod

Seeking family members of F/O George L. MacLeod, son of L. George and Marion L. MacLeod, Halifax. Date of birth circa 1922. He graduated from Dalhousie with a BCom. He was an RCAF pilot, 21st Squadron. His Mosquito aircraft crashed near Neerijse, Belgium, Sept. 29,1944, and he is buried in Leopoldsburg War Cemetery, Belgium.

Please contact: Donald R. Mac-Leod, RVP, Clan MacLeod Society of Canada, 902-864-6603; e-mail nova.don@ns.sympatico.ca

In 2006, I was living in California. My cousin, Mollie Cameron, in Halifax spotted ithe notice and phoned me. I called the number and talked to Don MacLeod, who had inserted the notice on behalf of of a Belgian aviation writer, Dirk Vander Hulst. I then emailed Dirk., who had unearthed some evidence of interest to me. and I joined him in his investigation, as did Colin Wiggins, a nephew of the navigator. We obtained information from various government agencies, which would provide it only to next off Kin.

Our efforts would lead to the eventual proof that my older brother, Dewar and his navigator, F/L Wiggins, who had died **sixty-two years earlier** while with the RCAF in Europe, had actually lost their lives to **"Friendly Fire"**.

Over a period of 8-9 months:

> We contacted the British Air Ministry, RAF Museum and Canadian Archives, among others. We traced the history of that particular Mosquito aircraft by contacting the manufacturer, deHavilland), We found that a Court of Inquiry had been held in March, 1945 and we obtained those record.

> We located the pilot of the other aircraft and communicated with him.

From: Dirk Vander Hulst
To: Don MacLeod, head of the Clan MacLeod Society
Sent: Thursday, July 6, 2006, 10:09 a.m.
Subject: G. D. Macleod of Halifax, Nova Scotia

Dear Sir,

My name is Dirk Vander Hulst, and I'm writing you from Belgium in the hopes you and the Clan MacLeod Society of Halifax can help me. I'm looking for living relatives of Flying Officer George Dewar MacLeod of Halifax, Nova Scotia, Canada.

His plane, a De Havilland Mosquito, came down in the Belgian village of Neerijse, which is situated about twenty kilometers east of Brussels, on September 29, 1944.

I intend to write an article about the fate of George Dewar MacLeod and his crewmate, Flying Officer Alan Charles Wiggins, for *Huldenbergs Heemblad,* which is the periodical of the local society for history and folklore of Huldenberg and its surrounding villages. One of the villages surrounding Huldenberg is Neerijse.

Yours sincerely,

Dirk Vander Hulst

From: Donald MacLeod, Clan MacLeod Society of Halifax
To: Dirk Vander Hulst
Sent: Thursday, July 6, 2006, 2:52 p.m.
Subject: Fwd: G. D. Macleod of Halifax, Nova Scotia

Dear Mr. Vander Hulst:

This will acknowledge my receipt of your e-mail dated July 6 regarding the late F/O George Dewar MacLeod of Halifax.

I have requested that the Canadian Department of National Defense's historical unit assist you in your search for information on this chap.

There are quite a number of MacLeods living in Halifax. I will do my best to assist you by searching birth, baptism, marriage, and death records at the public archives of Nova Scotia in an effort to determine if any of F/O MacLeod's relatives are still living. I will begin with the senior members of the Clan MacLeod Society of Halifax and move on from there.

Whatever archival and/or other information I might find will be posted or e-mailed to you.

It is also quite possible that he, like me, was born in the Cape Breton Island portion of Nova Scotia, so I will also contact a genealogist friend in that area of the province on this matter.

If possible, would you kindly keep me informed if you are able to proceed with your work?

As a member of the Clan MacLeod Society and a former member of the RCAF who served for two years (1954-1956) in Metz, Paris, and Baden-Sollingen (near Baden-Baden), I have an added interest.

Yours truly,

Donald MacLeod,
Clan MacLeod Society of Halifax
Clan MacLeod Societies of Canada

From: <nova.don@ns.sympatico.ca>
To: "dirk vander hulst" <vanderhulstdirk@yahoo.com>
Sent: Friday, July 07, 2006 7:26 PM
Subject: Re: G.D. MacLeod+photograph

Dear Mr. vander Hulst:

My apologies for referring to you as a Nederlander and not a Belgian and a Flemish Belgian at that. I trust the bureaucrats in Ottawa will notice my error when they read your address on a copy your email.

I am not very good at working computerized photographic programs, but will find some method of enlarging the passport photograph of either Mr. MacLeod or Mr. Wiggins. This way I can get a closer look at him. At first glance, I would suggest from the facial features, it may be Mr. MacLeod. If so, it might be a great asset in your quest for information.

I trust that I shall locate some of his relatives, hopefully alive.

My wife and I are involved in the Halifax Highland Games tomorrow, so I will not be able to go to the Public Archives of Nova Scotia for some days. We are also preparing for a visit to Scotland beginning on July 22nd. I will manage to get some time in at the Archives before our departure date. With the number of MacLeod families in Nova Scotia, it will be a challenge, but nonetheless a worthwhile challenge.

Kindest Regards

Donald ("Don") MacLeod

Dear Mr. Vander Hulst:

Great news! I published a small article in the *Halifax Herald* newspaper this week, and today I received a response from F/O MacLeod's brother in California, Dr. James MacLeod. Apparently his cousin, Mary Cameron, who lives in a seniors' home in Halifax, read the article and called Dr. MacLeod.

I have described the photograph to Dr. MacLeod, and it appears Dewar had blond, wavy hair, so this might be his photograph. He has asked if I would also take a copy of your e-mails and the photograph to his cousin here in Halifax. She is in her upper eighties.[1]

His cousin is Mary Cameron, better known as Mollie.

Dr. MacLeod, who was also serving in the RCAF at that time, flew with his brother in that mosquito bomber only ten days before George Dewar took off on a bombing mission to, I believe he said, the Ruhr Valley. Dr. MacLeod says they called him Dewar.

Yours truly,

Donald ("Don") MacLeod

---

[1]   She's actually ninety-five.

From: Dirk Vander Hulst
To: Don MacLeod
Sent: Tuesday, July 18, 2006 6:51 a.m.

Dear Mr. MacLeod,

My congratulations—that really is good news! I didn't expect an answer that soon. I'll try to e-mail Dr. MacLeod, and I'll send him a letter as a backup. I'll also write Mary Cameron to thank her and to inform her about my quest.

Many, many thanks!

Dirk Vander Hulst
July 20, 2006

Dear Mr. Vander Hulst,

I am very much interested in being made aware of your investigations into the fate of my brother, Dewar. What a fortunate combination of circumstances, including Mr. Don MacLeod's immediate cooperation, my cousin's alertness in spotting the note in the newspaper, and your persistence in searching out witnesses. Above all, I am amazed at the thoughtfulness of your "little old lady," who noted the names of the fliers when she was only seventeen, and most amazingly, kept those names for the next sixty-two years! This little old man, who was eighteen at the time, admires her presence of mind.

I will be happy to provide you with any information you wish—as little or as much as you wish.

I look forward to hearing from you.

James MacLeod

Thursday, July 20, 2006, 11:47 a.m.

Dear Dr. MacLeod,

It really is a fortunate combination of circumstances! Less than twenty days have passed since I first saw his picture and heard his name from that little old lady. Although the incident happened twenty-six years before I was born, I'm very eager to learn more about Dewar.

Recently, out of a historical and personal interest, I started looking for airmen whose aircraft had crashed in my neck of the wood during the Second World War, lest their names be forgotten by the people of Huldenberg and its surrounding villages, like Neerijse. I try to trace their individual fate through official records, by speaking with local witnesses, or by contacting the airmen themselves, when they are still alive, or their next of kin.

Since each year the numbers of veteran airmen and local witnesses are shrinking, I realize it is time to carry out such a project before it is too late. Many cases that happened close to where I live remain unsolved, but I hope this will not be the case for your brother's.

While I was interviewing the elderly people of Huldenberg, the name of a street in Neerijse called Koestraat kept turning up. They all stated that the airmen who had died in the Koestraat were Canadian and had a provisional grave on that same street. They recalled the airmen were buried near a verge that nowadays constitutes the natural limit of a pasture near the Koestraat (translation: Cow Street).

This all changed on Sunday, July 2, 2006, when I had the opportunity to talk to Mr. Roeykens, who lives in a newly built house on the Koestraat No. 2. I asked him if he was ever informed that a Canadian aircraft had crashed in the field bordering his house during WWII. The man had never heard of such a story. While we were talking, an elderly man named Mr. Van Beneden was peeping over his garden fence. Mr. Roeykens noticed him and he asked him whether he had ever heard of a crash in the Koestraat. He replied that he had heard this story from his wife. He immediately called his wife outside, who was named Mrs. Van Beneden-De Keyser.

De Keyser is her maiden name. She was born in 1927. She told me the crash happened around 2:00 or 3:00 a.m., while it was still dark. She still remembers that typical howling noise of an aircraft that went down. After the plane hit the ground, it set fire to the bushes in the area. What was left of the aircraft totally burned out. She was told this was always the case with Mosquito planes because they were made out of wood. Because there were fires everywhere—even farther in the distance—her family feared the straw roof of their house might catch fire, which luckily didn't happen. Fires were probably started by the exploding ammunition and the scattered fragments of the plane.

The whole incident made a strong impression on her, and she wrote down the names of the unfortunate men in her notebook. She remembered their family names and pronounced them as MacLeod and Wiggins. I wrote them down, and she confirmed my spelling. Then she disappeared into the house and reappeared with a worn little passport photograph.

"This was one of them. I don't know whether it's MacLeod or Wiggins. I do know for certain it's one of them because one of them had the same wavy hair as the man in the picture," she said.

I was astonished and touched when I was confronted with the portrait of the young man, who had died only a few feet away from where we were standing.

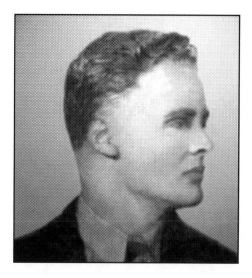

Is this a photograph of your brother?

We walked a few hundred yards down the Koestraat toward the field where your brother and Flying Officer Wiggins were found. She pointed to a verge that was situated higher up the slope, near a pasture. "Their bodies were temporarily buried at the foot of that very verge," she said. They were put in two separate coffins by members of the Belgian resistance, who stood guard over their graves for the next three days and nights.

Sometime afterward, the fliers were exhumed and eventually buried in a British military cemetery. A rumor persisted that one of the engines might still be buried in the cornfield. This rumor was confirmed by Mr. Vanbeneden. He told me that in the early years after the crash, horse-drawn plows didn't disturb the earth very deeply, but with modernization of agriculture, plows became heavier and were drawn by larger tractors, and the plow then hit the engines often.

According to the Record Operations Book (ORB) of No. 21 Sqn., their aircraft was Mosquito serial number PZ306, and according to aviation specialists and literature, your brother and Wiggins most likely fell to friendly fire or were shot down by Allied fire.

One particular author has your brother's Mosquito, serial number NT179, listed as shot down by a night-fighter Mosquito, serial number HK250, of No. 219 (RAF) Squadron. None of the above sources mention a crash location.

Because the real truth about what actually caused your brother's death and that of F/O Wiggins probably is hidden in documents held at The National Archives at Kew, United Kingdom, I contacted Mr. Cynrik De Decker, a Belgian aviation historian, who knows the holdings of The National Archives at Kew. I have contacted him several times in the past with regard to other unsolved mysteries in the area. He too is interested in your brother's case and will help me try to unveil the mystery that shrouds your brother's death. He is the vice president of the Belgian Aviation History Association (BAHA). They have an archaeological team (BAHAAT), and if the rumor about the engine never having been salvaged is true and the circumstances are favorable, they might be interested in unearthing it. Information about Cynrik De Decker, BAHA, and BAHAAT can be found on http://www.baha.be/index. htm and http://users.pandora.be/airwareurope/en/start_e.htm. The latter website is very interesting because it gives a good idea of what the association is all about.

As you see, different sources contradict one another. Is it because friendly-fire incidents are still a delicate matter?

Would it be possible for you to make a short biography of your brother? I'd also appreciate photographs showing your brother or you and your brother.

I've attached some photographs of the Koestraat, which I thought might interest you.

Yours truly,

Dirk Vander Hulst

The Koestraat (Cow St.), Neerijse

According to witnesses, the Mosquito came down right behind the wood stack.

The cornfield where one of the engines is still buried.

As a result of the impact or of the explosion(s) following the impact, several fragments of the Mosquito were projected into the fields and pastures situated on the left-hand side of the Koestraat. The bodies of MacLeod and Wiggins were also found on the left-hand side of the Koestraat.

VERGE WHERE THEY
WERE BURIED

SPOT WHERE
DEWAR AND ALAN
WERE FOUND

ENGINE BLOCK

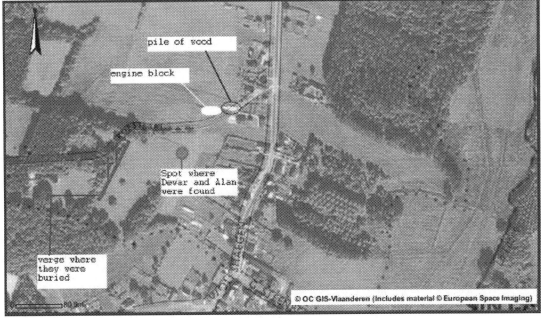

pile of wood

engine block

Spot where
Dewar and Alan
were found

verge where
they were
buried

© OC GIS-Vlaanderen (includes material © European Space Imaging)

Dear Mr. Vander Hulst,

The photograph you attached is of my brother, Dewar.

Dewar and I both grew up in Halifax. Dewar was four years older than me, and we were the only children. He graduated from Dalhousie University at age nineteen and a few months later enlisted in the RCAF.

About a year later, he graduated as a pilot, was commissioned as a pilot officer (subsequently a flying officer), and became a flying instructor at the SFTS (Service Flying Training School) in St. Hubert, in the Province of Quebec (near Montreal). In early 1944, he entered training on Mosquitoes prior to operational flying in England and was eventually attached to the RAF and posted to #21 Squadron.

I was a bomb aimer in the RCAF and made a short visit to him at his base at Thorney Island. During that visit, he took me for a short flight. That was ten days before his death. Subsequently, I visited his squadron again to learn what I could.

I've had Dewar's ID photograph restored. If Rosa would like one, I'd like her to have it with my sincere thanks.

I've also attached some other photographs of Dewar, as you requested, and I've included one of Alan, Dewar's navigator.

Sincerely yours

James H. MacLeod

Dewar 1941

July 30, 2006

Dear Dr. MacLeod,

Thank you very much for the restored ID photo of your brother and for the other photos. The next time I see Rosa, I'll extend your thanks and give it to her.

Yours truly,

Dirk

August 1, 2006

Dear Dr. MacLeod,

I received your family history, and I'm most grateful to you for entrusting me with one of the important and decisive chapters in your life—your youth years and your great respect for your older brother and your father. It must have been difficult times for you and your mother losing both in such a short time.

It's stories like yours—personal stories—that help us understand the greater and deeper tragedy of war.

Very truly yours,

Dirk

Dear Mr. Vander Hulst,

I have one question: Why did you choose the MacLeod clan for your first line of inquiry?

I also have one observation: it's time we got on a first-name basis.

Sincerely,

Jamie MacLeod

August 13, 2006

Dear Jamie,

I came across the following website: http://www.dehavilland.ukf.net/mosquito. htm/. On the website I found a Mosquito production list appears showing the aircraft serial number, mark, squadron, and fate. NT179's fate is recorded:

> NT179, FBVI 21, Shot down by another intruder over Germany 29.9.44
> (FBVI = fighter-bomber Mark 6)

The list is based on the Air Britain volumes. The Air Britain volumes have been constructed from the official RAF aircraft movement cards (air ministry form 78). To be assured of the fate of NT179, I wrote the RAF Museum for a copy of the aircraft movement card of NT179.

Sincerely,

Dirk

August 24, 2006

Dear Jamie,

I regret to inform you that according to the air ministry form 1180 accident card, which I received from the Royal Air Force Museum London, your brother's aircraft was brought down by an Allied aircraft.

I attached copies of the form 1180 accident card, which were made from microfilm, together with the letter I received from the RAF Museum London. The accident card shows that MacLeod G. D. piloted Mosquito serial number NT179 on the night of September 28/29, 1944.

Here are some quotations from form 1180:

> A/C (aircraft) shot down by friendly A/C in mistake for a JU 88 (Junkers 88). A/C was not showing Resin (?) Light.

> IFF not switched on. Shot down by friendly fighter.

> IFF is the abbreviation for, "Identification, Friend or Foe." Airborne radio system emitting preset signal when queried.

Air Ministry Form 1180 was designed to record details of aircraft accidents so the causes could be analyzed and the resulting data used in accident prevention. Because of this, the following phrase included in form 1180 pertaining to NT179: "Every effort is being made to obtain night glasses for all air crew."

Today I received an e-mail from Colin Wiggins, the nephew of Alan Wiggins. Colin Wiggins lives in the United States and is very interested in the fate of his uncle Alan. He asked me for your contact information, which I gave him.

Kindest regards,

Dirk

⦿ ROYAL AIR FORCE museum

RAFM/32/6/GR

Mr. D.V. Hulst
Molenstraat 27
St-Joris-Weert
3051
Belgium   21st August 2006

Dear Mr. Hulst,

Thank you for your enquiry which was received on 27th July 2006. You wished to receive information relating to the loss of Fg Off George Dewar MacLeod and Fg Off Alan Charles Wiggins. Please find enclosed the Air Ministry Form 1180 Accident Card for the incident in which this aircraft was brought down by another Allied aircraft. Unfortunately the identity of the second aircraft involved is not recorded. The RAF Museum's (incomplete) set of World War Two combat reports does not contain a 219 Squadron report for the night of 28th/29th September 1944 so I am unable to provide any details about the possibility that MacLeod and Wiggins were shot down by HK250 as you suggest. A much more complete set of combat reports is held by the UK's National Archives, in the AIR 50 class of records. Contact details for The National Archives can be found on the enclosed RAF Museum guide to the research of RAF units. I hope that I have been able to assist you with your research.

Yours sincerely,

GUY REVELL
Assistant Curator
Department of Research & Information Services
guy.revell@rafmuseum.org

Royal Air Force Museum London
Grahame Park Way
London NW9 5LL
www.rafmuseum.org

T: 020 8205 2266
F: 020 8200 1751
london@rafmuseum.org

Registered charity no. 244708

Card — Aircraft Accident / Casualty Record (form)

Top section

DATE	28	9	44	UNIT	21 Sqdn	OP N	Op	G 2	2nd T.A.F	COMMAND

DIS. Cas/Md
78(X)G 23
FILE S.81083/44

A/C TYPE — MARK: Mosquito VI
ENG. TYPE SINGLE/PORT/O
PORT/1: Merlin XX · 441050 E
STBD/1: 664? · 440466 E

PLACE: In flight over enemy territory
R.A.F.
PEOPLE IN AIRCRAFT: 2   TOT: 2

FUNCTION	NAME, INITIALS, NATIONALITY	RANK	NUMBER	TOTAL SOLO Total · Time	NIGHT SOLO Total · Time	INST LINK	CAS.
Pilot	McLeod G.D. (Can)	F/O	J.25005	1693 · 90	136 · 21	'65	M

O.D.
311737?

Bottom section

ACC. CODE. NO. — FLIGHT — UNDER CARRIAGE — AIRFRAME — EXTERNAL — WEATHER

FLIGHT: M · N   DAY/NIGHT N   DUAL SOLO PILOTS   DUTY Ops — patrol duties over W. Germany
ACC.   HRS   DAY/NIGHT N   LIGHT Bright

1H — A/C shot down by friendly A/C in mistake for
a J.188. Officers not observing Battle Lights.

GOK
DK
EDK
U NK — IFF not switched on.
A (NK) — Shot down by friendly fighter.
X FF
W OK
SP. REC. RADAR — ADDITIONAL EVIDENCE — A.OC & NOC in C scene

Every effort is being made by civilian night officers
for all air crews.

BLAME AND DISCIP. ACTION

August 24, 2006

Dear Dirk,

Thanks for the most recent information. We did our grieving long ago, but this news is still a shock. I'm only glad our parents aren't here to cope with it.

I have just a couple of comments. First, they weren't the first to be shot down because the IFF was not switched on. Second, the term "Resin" and its significance are not familiar to me.

With my best wishes,

Jamie

Dear Dr. Macleod,

Mr. Vander Hulst has given me your e-mail address, at my request. My uncle, Flying Officer Alan Wiggins, was the navigator of the Mosquito piloted by your brother shot down almost sixty-two years ago.

Today Mr. Vander Hulst passed on the tragic revelation that this was the result of so-called friendly fire. He has done an incredible job of researching this awful affair, and I have begun furnishing him with what little I have in the way of photos, data, and recollections, as I am sure you have also.

If you would like to see any of this material, please let me know. I tried telephoning the number he gave me for you, but it was said to be disconnected!

Yours sincerely,

Colin Wiggins

Dear Mr. Wiggins,

Thanks for your e-mail yesterday. Yes, I would like very much to receive any pertinent material you may have. If you would like any I have, I'll be happy to send it to you.

Sincerely yours,

James MacLeod

Dear Jamie,

RAF Innsworth will probably be able to shed a light on Dewar's military service, his tragic loss, and the accident. Casualty inquiries can be made to RAF Innsworth. Their policy says, "Information about casualties is deemed to be personal; only enquiries in writing from or on behalf of next of kin can be considered."

Air Historical Branch (RAF) also maintains historical records relating to individual aircraft. Their website is: http://www.bbc.co.uk/ww2peopleswar/stories/79/a2313479.shtml

Dirk

Dear Jamie,

Many thanks for your e-mail and the review of your family history. Your brother must have had a phenomenal intellect to graduate from Dalhousie at nineteen years of age. I was almost nineteen when I finished at Abingdon School, and I went to Oxford a couple of months later. Dalhousie offered me a post at one point, but we decided to move to Vancouver and take up a post-doc position on the physics faculty at UBC.

With all good wishes,

Colin

Subject: The Priest's Letter
Date: Sunday, September 3, 2006, 7:30 a .

Dear Jamie,

As I mentioned previously, I have found a battered copy of what was probably a handwritten letter from the priest to my grandmother. It looks as though it was treasured and carried around for years in a pocket, wallet, or pocketbook.

My wife has retyped it for clarity, and a copy is attached. Reference is made in the last paragraph to the visit of a nephew, but in fact this is a grandson, Craftsman Philip Jones, my cousin. I learned a few days ago that he was hospitalized with a heart condition. He should be released to his home midweek, but I am reluctant to press him for information under the circumstances.

My son has rendered the RAF Museum letter and the crash docs into .pdf form. I will send you a copy if that would be of interest.

Enjoy the Labor Day weekend. The sun is at last appearing here!

Colin

MONT-CESAR ABBEY, LOUVAIN.
April 2, 1945.

Madam,

I had the honor to be called upon to assist your son on the occasion of the fatal accident in which he lost his life. It was on St. Michael's Day, September 29, at about 2:45 a.m. The accident happened near Neeryssche, at a place called Wolfshaegen. You may find it on a map, situated between the two villages of Neeryssche and Huldenberg, fifteen miles or so southeast from Brussels, ten miles from Louvain, and about five miles to the right of the main road Brussels-Louvain.

On that very night, I suddenly woke up to the sound of a plane that seemed to be in difficulty. Soon afterward a second plane twirled round the place at high speed. There were two or three rounds of machine-gun fire and almost immediately, a crash. The whole business didn't last more than two minutes. When I came outside, I saw a huge fire almost in front of my house, and as I came nearer, I found a Mosquito fighter-bomber ablaze. It had exploded before it crashed at about roof level. Apparently the pilot had tried to land in the open field but had been chased by a German fighter. The plane was hit by his gunfire and collapsed. The German fled away having fired some SOS signals, as he was bound to do.

We tried to give assistance to the crew of the wrecked plane, but owing to the heat, it was quite impossible to approach. After a few minutes, however, and at a distance of about a hundred yards, we discovered the bodies of the two pilots. They had been projected by the violent explosion and doubtlessly had been killed instantaneously. Whether they had been hit by the gunfire or killed by the explosion itself, it was impossible to ascertain. Since both pilots had fractures of their skulls and their spines broken, death must have been sudden and painless. We found the enlistment card of your son with the identity disk of his fellow pilot, which gave us the most valuable information.

I went to the nearest post of the British Army, which happened to be a unit of the airborne troops just returned from Arnhem. Meanwhile the two bodies were guarded by a squad of Belgian soldiers.

With the assistance of the Rev. H. L. Stapley (Nesta, 1, Lynch Crescent, Winscombe, Somerset), chaplain of the airborne division, and a score of men from this unit, we buried your son and his unfortunate comrade with military honors. A large crowd, deeply moved, attended while the chaplain performed the ceremony and had the usual prayers said.

The grave of your son is situated halfway up a bushy hill. Sympathizing neighbors keep the tomb flowered and often say a prayer for the unfortunate heroes and their families.

I handed your son's identity card together with the other items we found on the spot to the Rev. Stapley. I expect they were forwarded with an official and full account to the war office by whose care you must have been informed. The officer in charge of the Airborne division told me that after the war His Majesty's Government intends to establish large military cemeteries to group the bodies of those who have fallen away from the battle area, as is the case of your son.

As a Catholic priest, I said Holy Mass for the repose of your son's soul, and I asked the community of nuns, to which for the time being I acted as chaplain, to pray for him and for all those who would be grieved by his death. Your only comfort, of course, is to know that your son gave his life for his God, his king, and his country.

I shall always remember him. He was the first of those valiant British soldiers I was allowed to assist, unfortunately under very sad circumstances; but I cannot forget that he also gave his life for our liberation.

Your nephew, Cfn. P. Jones, told me how much Alan Charles loved his mother and how deeply affected you were by his death. I pray God would comfort you in His mercy and grant you strength to bear this trial serenely.

Yours sincerely,(signed)   D. ANSELM ROBBEYNS O.B.

Abbaye du Mont-Cesar, Louvain. (Belgium)

Dear Jamie and Colin,

I requested an estimate for document copies from The National Archives pertaining to the combat reports of No. 219 Squadron. According to the estimate I received from The National Archives, a copy of the combat reports of No. 219 Sqdn (National Archives reference AIR 50/84) for the night of September 28/29, 1944, can't be ordered. Strange?

Mr. Bill Carp a British aviation expert and author, offered me his help and will try to check the combat reports of No. 219 Sqdn at The National Archives, Kew.

Dirk

Dear Dirk and Colin,

Attached are copies of my letter to Innsworth, their reply, and copies of Dewar's service record as well as all of the RCAF letters.

I also attach the response to my application to Library and Archives Canada.

My best wishes to you both,

Jamie

Sept. 7, 2006

PMA IM1b (RAF)
Room 5
Building 248A
Personnel Management Agency
Innsworth
Gloucester GL3 1EZ
England

Dear Sirs,

Re: F/O George Dewar MacLeod, RCAF J22008

As his next of kin, I am requesting copies of the records of the above airman, my brother, who was killed while attached to the R.A.F. I am particularly interested in any evidence of his death by "friendly fire".

I enclose a copy of a newspaper account as proof of our relationship.

My cheque in the amount of £30.00 is also enclosed.

I thank you for your consideration.

Yours very truly,

James H. MacLeod, M.D.

ROYAL AIR FORCE
PERSONNEL MANAGEMENT AGENCY
ROYAL AIR FORCE INNSWORTH
GLOUCESTER GL3 1EZ

Telephone:	(Direct)	01452 712612 Ext 7906
	(RAFTN)	95471 Ext 7906
	(Fax)	(01452) 510877 or 95471 6268

Dr J H MacLeod MD
708 N Hillcrest Road
Beverly Hills
CA 90210-3517
USA

Your Reference:

Our Reference: 65736PW

Date: 12 September 2006

Dear Dr MacLeod

Thank you for your recent letter, and enclosed cheque.

I have pleasure in enclosing a copy of the officer's record of service in the Royal Canadian Air Force, while serving alongside the Royal Air Force, for your late brother Flying Officer George Dewar MacLeod.

Details of his former service can be obtained by writing to the following address: **Personnel Records, National Archives of Canada, 395 Wellington Street, Ottawa, Ontario, Canada, K1A 0N3.**

As the enclosed record is incomplete, it has been decided on this occasion to waive the search fee of £30.00. The cheque is, therefore, returned for you disposal.

I hope that you will find the information provided of interest and assistance.

Yours sincerely

P Williams

P WILLIAMS (Mrs)
PMA IM1b1b

NAME GEORGE DEWAR MACLEOD

Father's Name
and Address: LAUCHLIN GEORGE MACLEOD

Date and Place of Birth 7-1-22, HALIFAX, N.S.
(See Birth Certificate).

Number T92008

Date of Gazette and Subsequent Promotions			Rewards and H. in D.		Causes of Resignation, etc.			Where Recruited, Languages, and other special
te of Gazette.	Rank.	With Effect From.	Reward.	Authority.	Subject.	Remarks.	Result.	
2 30	Granted Comm. as P/O RCAF (R.32.)	18-12-42	Pilots Badge	18-12-42				Enrolled High School Senior Matric University, Dalhousie, Subject Commerce
	P/O		C.V.S.M.	15-1-44				
	Pilot	18-6-43						Civilian (Student) Student
								Religion United Church

	Previous Service.					Aircraft flown Moth, Harvard, Yale, Cornells, Venturas
thority.	Appointment.	With Effect From.	Authority.	Appointment.	With Effect From.	
2 30	RCAF R137501 Enlisting	18-10-41				

PREVIOUS SERVICE COUNTING TOWARD
RETIREMENT ON RETIRED PAY.
Years. Days.
UNITS.
Other Rank Service ...
Warrant Officer Service ...
Commissioned Service ...
TOTAL
OF WHICH___YEARS___DAYS COUNT
TOWARDS RETIRED PAY.

Date of Retirement.

Special Notes.

MACLEOD   G D   Name and Initials.

Name and Address
of next-of-kin: MRS. L.G. MACLEOD

Relationship MOTHER 31 PRESTON ST. HALIFAX, N.S.

Date and Place of Marriage   S
(See Marriage Certificate).

Name of Wife

SENIORITY BOARDS.					MOVEMENTS.					MOVEMENTS.				
Disciplinary and Date of Commencement	Date and Place of Board.	Classifi- cation.	Date of Next Board	Remarks.	Authority.	Unit.	Acct.	With Effect From.	Special Remarks of Duties.	Authority.	Unit.	Acct.	With Effect From.	Special of I
					Est 0222 Emb. Halifax Disemb. U.K. W/S/Sgt/Sgt		29.6.44 7.7.44	Emb. Halifax 17.4.44 Disemb. Pilot Duty at Rep. Dep (overseas)						

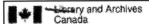 Library and Archives
Canada

Bibliothèque et Archives
Canada

2006/08/29

Our file   Notre référence
Q-06/07-1-44122

JAMES MACLEOD
706 N. HILLCREST RD
BEVERLY HILLS CALIFORNIA 90210
UNITED STATES

This letter is to acknowledge receipt of your request. Thank you for your interest in the Library and Archives Canada. Please be assured that we will respond as soon as possible.

Due to the large number of inquiries received, we are currently experiencing delays in our response time. We will provide you with a reply in six months, or sooner, as our workload permits.

Priority service is given to people who require documentation to prove that they qualify for pensions, allowances, claims and other benefits, therefore, these types of requests should be clearly identified.

Should you have access to the Internet and you are interested in learning more about our records, please consult our web site www.collectionscanada.ca. If you need to contact us, please quote the above file number.

ATIP & PERSONNEL RECORDS DIVISION
Fax: 1-(613) 947-8456

La présente lettre est pour accuser réception de votre demande de renseignements adressée à Bibliothèque et Archives Canada. Nous vous remercions de nous avoir écrit et nous allons traiter votre demande aussitôt que possible.

Vu le nombre élevé de demandes reçues, nous éprouvons actuellement un retard dans notre temps de réponse. Nous vous ferons parvenir une réponse d'ici six mois ou plus tôt selon notre charge de travail.

Nous accordons la priorité aux personnes qui ont besoin de certains documents pour prouver qu'elles sont admissibles à des pensions, à des indemnités, à des allocations ou à d'autres types de prestations, par conséquent, ces demandes doivent être clairement identifiées.

Si vous avez accès à l'Internet et vous désirez obtenir de plus amples renseignements concernant nos documents, vous pouvez consulter notre site Web au www.collectionscanada.ca. Veuillez vous assurer d'inscrire le numéro de référence ci-haut si vous devez communiquer avec nous.

DIVISION DE L'AIPRP ET DES DOCUMENTS DU PERSONNEL
Télécopieur: 1-(613) 947-8456

Canadä

October 17, 2006

Dear Dirk,

Attached are copies of all the RCAF letters from 1944 onward, as you requested.

Sincerely,

Jamie

ADDRESS REPLY TO:

THE SECRETARY,

DEPARTMENT OF NATIONAL DEFENCE FOR AIR,

OTTAWA, ONTARIO.

OUR FILE   J22068   (R.O.4)

REF. YOUR.

DATED

ROYAL CANADIAN AIR FORCE

AIR MAIL

OTTAWA, Canada, 25th October, 1944.

Mr. L.G. MacLeod,
31 Preston Street,
Halifax, Nova Scotia.

Dear Mr. MacLeod:

It is with deep regret that I must confirm our recent telegram informing you that your son, Flying Officer George Dewar MacLeod, previously reported missing, is now reported killed on Active Service.

Advice has now been received from the Royal Canadian Air Force Casualties Officer, Overseas, that your son lost his life during air operations at approximately 3:00 A.M. on September 29th, 1944, and was buried in Belgium. Further burial particulars are expected from Overseas, and when received they will be communicated to you immediately.

I realise that this news has been a great shock to you, and I offer you my deepest sympathy. May the same spirit which prompted your son to offer his life give you courage.

Yours sincerely,

(J.A. Sully)
Air Vice-Marshal,
Air Member for Personnel.

ADDRESS REPLY TO:

THE SECRETARY.
DEPARTMENT OF NATIONAL DEFENCE FOR AIR.
OTTAWA. ONTARIO.

OUR FILE   J22006 (R.O.4)

REF. YOUR ....

DATED ....

ROYAL CANADIAN AIR FORCE

A I R   M A I L   OTTAWA, Canada, 13th November, 1944.

Mr. L.G. MacLeod,
31 Preston Street,
Halifax, Nova Scotia.

Dear Mr. MacLeod:

      Further to the letter to you dated October 25th
from Air Vice-Marshal J.A. Sully, a report has been received from
Overseas containing additional particulars concerning your son's
death.

      The message states your son's aircraft crashed
at Neeryssche, Belgium, at approximately 3:00 A.M. on September 29th,
1944, and both occupants were instantly killed. Neeryssche is
located near Louvain, Belgium.

      Additional information concerning his grave has
been requested from Overseas and as soon as this is forthcoming
it will be forwarded to you immediately.

      May I again assure you and the members of your
family of my deepest sympathy.

        Yours sincerely,

        R.C.A.F. Casualty Officer,
        for Chief of the Air Staff.

R.C.A.F., G. 32P
5000—1-44 (1372)
H.Q. 885-G-321

C
O
P
Y

Our file J.22008(RC4)
Ref.Your _____
Dated _____

The Secretary,
Dept. of National Defence for Air,
Ottawa, Ont.

R O Y A L   C A N A D I A N   A I R   F O R C E

Ottawa, Ontario,
22nd May 1945.

Mr. A. G. MacLeod,
31 Preston Street,
Halifax, N.S.

Dear Mr. MacLeod;

     As a result of the investigation made by Overseas
Headquarters, the information has now been received from
Belgium regarding the location of your son's grave. This report
states that your son and F/O Wiggins, the other member of the
crew, were buried near the scene of the crash. A British Chaplain,
Reverend H.L.Stapley and 21 Belgian soldiers officiated at the
funeral. The Graves Registration authorities will, as soon as
possible, remove your son and F/O Wiggins to an established
cemetery where they will be laid at rest with others of the
Armed Forces. When this is done, you will be notified.

     If you wish to communicate with Rev. Stapley, his
address is:

           Reverend H. L. Stapley,
           Nasta,
           1 Lynch Crescent,
           Winscombe, Somerset.

     May I again offer you my deep sympathy in your
great loss.

           Yours sincerely,

       (SIGNED) JOHN WESTMAN F/O
       R.C.A.F. Casualty Officer
       for Chief of the Air Staff.

THE SECRETARY,
DEPARTMENT OF NATIONAL DEFENCE FOR AIR.
OTTAWA, ONTARIO.

OUR FILE .... (BO)

REF. YOUR ....

DATED ....

ROYAL CANADIAN AIR FORCE

OTTAWA, Canada, 10th August, 1948.

Mrs. E.L. MacLeod,
31 Preston St.,
Halifax, N.S.

Dear Mrs. MacLeod:

Please find enclosed a photograph
which has been received from Overseas, of the grave of
your son, Flying Officer George Omar MacLeod.

Cemeteries are being handed over progressively to the Imperial War Graves Commission, of
which Canada is a member, who are entrusted with the
perpetual maintenance of the resting places of all our
Fallen, and who will beautify the graves and surround-
ings, and erect a permanent headstone at each grave.

It is not necessary for you to contact
the Commission. Any discrepancy as to rank, etc., which
may appear on the temporary cross shown in the enclosed
photograph, will appear correctly on the permanent headstone.

Yours sincerely,

(W.A. Dicks)
Wing Commander,
for Chief of the Air Staff.

Encl.

October 18, 2006

Dear Jamie and Colin,

Regarding XXX Sqdn

Flt. Lt. John Doe of XXX Sqdn[2] was probably responsible for the deaths of Dewar and Charles. It was the English researcher/writer, Bill Carp, who recently pointed out to me that the culprit was probably John Doe. Bill got the information from a fellow researcher/writer named Peter Smith. Here's Bill Carp e-mailed me:

> Now, please do not quote me (yet), but I believe the information came from Peter Smith (the NZ writer/researcher) who interviewed John Doe some years ago. I will give you his e-mail address in the hope that he might help you.

John Doe applied for a short service commission in 1938 and started flying.

He began training in January 1939 and joined 141 Squadron in October. The squadron had no aircraft of its own at the time but gradually formed two flights: one of Gladiators and the other of Blenheims. In March 1940, 141 began to receive Defiants, becoming operational on June 3.

On July 19, 1940, twelve Defiants were ordered to patrol twenty miles south of Folkestone. Three had engine trouble, and only nine made their way to the patrol area. Surprised by a force of Me 109s, three of the rear four Defiants were shot down in flames before they could take any defensive action. The fourth, flown by Plt. Off. John Doe, was also shot down but did not catch fire and crash landed at sea four miles south of Dover.

His aircraft sank, but he escaped. After fifteen minutes, he was picked up with severe head wounds requiring hospitalization. His gunner did not survive. John Doe rejoined the squadron in late October after three months of sick leave and completed a tour of two hundred operational hours there.

---

[2]   The squadron number and pilot responsible have been withheld.

On November 1, 1941, John Doe joined an RCAF Squadron of Beaufighters. He was promoted to acting squadron leader the next year and joined 488 Squadron as a flight commander. Once his second tour was completed in November 1942, John Doe was posted to HQ 13 Group, Newcastle, and took a course at RAF Staff College while there.

On January 1, 1944, he went to an OTU and on April 25 took a refresher course on Beaufighters and then joined a Mosquito Squadron as a supernumerary. (He was with this squadron when he shot down Dewar's plane.)He returned to 488 in late October as flight commander. The squadron moved across to the continent on November 15, 1944. Operating from Amiens-Glisy, Mosquito destroyed a FW 190 in December. Within days, he was forced to make a one-engine landing at Brussels-Melsbroek, after being damaged by antiaircraft fire. A day later, his aircraft was destroyed on the ground there by a German strafing attack.

John Doe was with 488 until it was disbanded in April 1945. He returned to England and was posted to Air Ministry, Directorate of Organisational Establishments. He received a Mention in Despatches (1.1.46), returned to New Zealand in March 1947, and went on the reserve on June 12. Offered a permanent commission in September, John Doe returned to the UK in 1948. He held a series of appointments and commands prior to his retirement on June 14 1965 as a wing commander, retaining the rank of group captain.

The information mentioned below with regard to John Doe was extracted from the RAF Commands forum: http://www.rafcommands.com/cgi-bin/dcforum/dcboard.cgi?az=printer_format&om=5332&forum=DCForumID6.

Original Message

"Pilot and Backhouse"
Posted by Hugh on September 6, 2004 at 10:03 a.m.

F/L J. D. Pilot and F/O J. W. Backhouse were pilot and navigator in No. XXX Squadron in September 1944. Does anyone have a 1944 air force list providing their service numbers?

Messages in this discussion

"RE: PILOT and Backhouse"
Posted by Errol (Guest) on September 6, 2004 at 11:30 a.m.

Hugh,

Found 116943 Backhouse, J. W., "released" in the October 1946 AFL. He's very likely same as your 1944 man. No sign of John Doe, however.

Errol

"RE: John Doe and Backhouse"
Posted by marks on September 6, 2004 at 3:35 p.m.

Hugh,

I was checking *Men of the Battle of Britain* by Wynn and found 41841 P/O J. Doe.

APO 1.4.39 PO 23.10.39 FO 23.10.40 FL 23. 10.41 SL 1.7.45
SL 1.8.47 WC 1.1.54 Ret RAF G/C 14.6.65

Dob 14.6.1918 Dunedin.

His later service indicates he transferred to RNZAF 1.1.1944. Went to 51 OTU Bedford on April 25 for a refresher course on Beaufighters and then joined XXX Sqn (Mosquito) at Bradwell Bay as supernumerary. He returned to XXX Sqn in late October as a flight commander.

I have more info if you want it.

All the best,

Mark

RE: J. Doe and Backhouse
Posted by mailto:*Errol (Guest) on September 6, 2004 at 9:42 p.m.*

I've already drawn this to Hugh's attention by e-mail but for others on the board who are following this thread:

> Excerpt from *By Such Deeds—Honours and Awards in the Royal New Zealand Air Force 1923-1999*:
>
> PIlot, Squadron Leader John Doe, mid, (bbc).
>
> NZ2177; Born Dunedin, 14 Jun 1918; RAF 23 Jan 1939 to 31 Dec 1943, 41841; RNZAF 1 Jan 1944 to 12 Jun 1947; Pilot.
>
> Later John Doe mid, RAF 12 Feb 1948 to 14 Jun 1965, 41841.
>
> Citation Mention in Despatches (NY1946): For distinguished service. Served as a Flt Cdr with 488 Sqn RNZAF.

Errol

"RE: Doe and Backhouse"
Posted by Terry on September 8, 2004 at 1:42 a.m.

Hugh, this is more than you asked for, but from the LG:

1323364 Sgt John Webster Backhouse was commissioned as a PO (116943) wef 20 Oct 42, promoted FO wef 20 Apr 43 and FL wef 20 Oct 44.

Regards,

Terry

Other Documents

I received the following documents, which I'll send to you both by surface mail:

- A photocopy of air ministry form 78 (aircraft movement card) for De Havilland Mosquito aircraft serial number NT179 (source: RAF Museum London).

- A photocopy of air ministry form 540 (summary of events) from the Operations Record Book of No. 21 Squadron RAF, for September 1944 (source: The National Archieves, Kew, UK, Reference AIR 27/264).

- A copy of air ministry form 541 (detail of work carried out) from the Operations Record Book of No. 21 Squadron RAF for the night of September 28/29, 1944. (source: The National Archives, Kew, UK, Reference AIR 27/264).

War Graves Commission

I haven't received word yet from the Commonwealth.

War Graves Commission about the different places Dewar and Charles were buried.

My best wishes,

Dirk

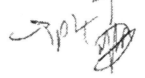

Dr. James MacLeod Md
706 North Hillcrest Road.
Beverley Hills, California, 90210-3517
U.S.A.

Sint-Joris-Weert, 18 October 2006

Dear Jamie,

Please find enclosed the following documents:

- A letter from the RAF Museum, dated 25 September 2006, with regard to Air Ministry Form 78 (Aircraft Movement Card) for Mosquito aircraft serial number NT179
- A photocopy of Air Ministry Form 78 (Aircraft Movement Card) for De Havilland Mosquito aircraft serial number NT179.
- A photocopy of Air Ministry Form 540 (Summary of Events) from the Operations Record Book of No. 21 Squadron RAF, for September 1944 (source: The National Archieves, Kew, UK, Reference AIR 27/264).
- A copy of Air Ministry Form 541 (Detail of work carried out) from the Operations Record Book of No. 21 Squadron RAF for the night of September 28/29, 1944, (source: The National Archieves, Kew, UK, Reference AIR 27/264).

Remarks:

Abbreviations used in Air Ministry Form 78 (Aircraft Movement Card).
10 MU ~ 10 Maintenance Unit
417 ARF ~ 417 Aircraft Repair Flight
CAT E ~ Damage Category E, meaning aircraft is a write-off
FB ~ Operational loss
CAS/ 406 ~ This reference also appears on Air Ministry Form 1180 (Accident Card)

Air Ministry Form 540 (Summary of Events)
28.9.44 'Tonight the Squadron covered railways Rhene-Munster-Hannum ...'
I couldn't find Hannum on the map. Hannum is probably a typo, I believe the German city of Hamm was meant.

Air Ministry Form 541 (Detail of work carried out):
Why wasn't the time up of Mosquito NT179 (F/O MacLeod and F/O Wiggins) registered? The time up of the eleven other Mossies was carefully noted. It can't be a coincidence, obviously 21 Squadron 'covered-up' this friendly fire incidents.

With my best wishes.

Dirk Vander Hulst

Mailing address
DIRK VANDER HULST
MOLENSTRAAT 27
3051 SINT-JORIS-WEERT
BELGIUM
E-mail address:
vanderhulst.dirk@yahoo.com

ROYAL
AIR FORCE **museum**

RAFM/32/6/SH

Mr. D. Vander Hulst,
Molenstraat 27,
3051 St-Joris-Weert,
Belgium

25 September 2006

Dear Mr. Vander Hulst,

Thank you for your enquiry, which we received on the 28 August.

Please find enclosed the movement card for Mosquito NT179.

I hope that this helps you with your research.

Yours Sincerely,

Stuart Hadaway
Assistant Curator
Department of Research and Information Services
stuart.hadaway@rafmuseum.org

Royal Air Force Museum London
Grahame Park Way
London NW9 5LL
www.rafmuseum.org

Type of Aircraft		Mark	R.A.F. Number
MOSQUITO.		VI.	NT. 179.

Contractor	Contract No.	Engine installed :—
DE·HAVILLAND. HATFIELD	555.	MERLIN 25. Maker's airframe No. :—

Unit or Cat'y/Cause	Station or Contractor	Date	Authority	4) or 4) Gp. Allot.
	10. MU.	26·4·	14/44. 20.	61476.
	417 A.R.F.	3·8·44	147	—
	21 Sqn	7.9.44	T.36	
CAT E.	EB	28.9.44	CRO/1404	

A.M. form 78

Place.	Date.	Time.	Summary of Events.	References to Appendices
Thorney Island	17.9.44		with the result that only five aircraft bombed the target the remainder bringing bombs back to base. Heavy flak was encountered and F/L Boulter failed to return.	
	18.9.44		Tonight the Squadron patrolled the railways from Groningen to Bremen and covered the Schaldt crossings. Weather was poor and little or no activity was seen. P/O Pollick crashed into a hill at Petersfield whilst breaking cloud on returning to base.	
	19.9.44		In the afternoon there was some formation practice. At night the Squadron patrolled the railways from Groningen to Bremen and covered the Schaldt crossings.	
	20.9.44		The Squadron Stood down tonight.	
	21.9.44		W/L Mussett and P/O Burrows returned to the Squadron having been missing since the 1st. August, 1944. The Squadron stood by until 23.00 hours when operations were cancelled.	
	22.9.44		More good news today F/L Taylor and P/O Johnston missing since the 31st. August, 1944 were reported back in this country. The Squadron stood down tonight.	
	23.9.44		Bad weather curtailed operations tonight, but also a few crews managed to get away early to attack railways in Wesel-Osnabruck and Rheine-Emmin areas.	
	24.9.44		Air to ground firing practice in the afternoon. Weather again was very poor with a very low cloud base in the target area. Nevertheless the Squadron covered targets in the Schaldt area, Railways at Wesel-Osnabruck, Luther-Rheine-Osnabruck. Little or no activity was seen.	
	25.9.44		Poor weather again tonight - low cloud and bad visibility in rain. Targets were in the same area as last night. Little or no activity was seen.	
	26.9.44		There was a wing stand down tonight.	
	27.9.44		Tonight the Squadron covered the Schaldt crossings and railways Wesel-Munster-Osnabruck.	
	28.9.44		Tonight the Squadron covered railways Rheine-Munster -Hamm and a small area west of the battle line. P/O McLeod and P/O Wiggins failed to return from this operation.	
	29.9.44		There was a wing stand down tonight, on the occasion of a dance in the officers mess, given as a farewell party prior to our expected move to the continent.	
	30.9.44		As were all very sorry to-day to say goodbye to two old and very popular members of the Squadron our C.O. W/C Dennis DSO DFC & Bar and S/L "Sock" Hunter DFC DFM. W/O Hale DFC returns to command.	

[signature]
Wing Commander, Commanding,
No. 21 Squadron, R.A.F.

SECRET

DETAIL OF WORK CARRIED OUT

By ..... 21 Squadron ....

For the Month of ... September 19.44

Aircraft Type & Number	Crew	Duty	Time		Details of Sortie or Flight
			Up	Down	
Mosquito VI NT 197	S/L J. Murray F/L MB Allen F/L J. Potter	Overlord	20.15	23.15	Abandoned unable to jettison starboard tank.
LR 304	F/O G. Jordan F/S W. Halton		21.30	00.57	Bombed railway at S.1365 - n.r.s.
MM 903	F/O E. McOmish F/O V. Carlisle		22.15	02.45	Bombed lights in wood-lights doused.
NT 178	F/O R. Ingram F/O M. Balcot F/O A.G. Higgins		23.25	03.00	Strafed train-train stopped and slight smoke plus came
LR 348	F/O S. Baynt F/O J. Dobson F/O Kv. Finder				Failed to return
MM 905	F/O L. Elkington F/O J. Hopman		22.30	03.30	Strafed trucks burning on railway
LR 277	F/O J. Harbin		21.00	00.30	Bombed and strafed 4 mot-fire started but bombs overshot
MM 888	S/L R.B. Waldroid F/O Thompson		22.10	02.55	No suitable target found to attack.
LR 353	F/O A.J. Towers		21.30	012.5	Bombed and strafed 12 /trucks-strikes seen
LR 162	F/O G. Hamilton A. Adams		22.30	02.00	Strafed fire in wood-n.r.s. Flares brought back.
LR 988	Sgt. L. Nicholas		23.00	02.30	Strafed large building - strikes seen.
			20.30	23.45	Bombed and strafed light railroad 4/5 mot. lights dou

[signature: Hale]

No. 21 Squadron, R. .. F.

October 21, 2006

Hello, Jamie and Colin,

I did some research regarding Peter Smith on the Internet and found he lives in New Zealand. I then consulted the New Zealand White Pages and found his contact information.

The exact data provided to me by Bill Carp in case one of you should contact Mr. Smith—is that on the night of September 28/29, 1944, Mosquito NT179 of 21 Squadron (RAF) was shot down in a friendly fire incident by Mosquito HK250 flown by Flt. Lt. John Doe, Pilot of XXX Squadron (RAF).

As ever,

Dirk

November 4, 2006

Dear Jamie and Colin,

The cornfield where the engine of Mosquito NT179 is believed to be buried has recently been harvested.

Tomorrow, November 5, 2006, Cynrik De Decker and members of the Belgian Aviation History Association Archaeology Team (BAHAAT) will search the field with the aid of metal detectors to try and pinpoint the engine's exact location.

I realize it's far too early to really speak of a cover up as there is insufficient proof at the moment. By cover up, I mean that all indications that might eventually lead to the identification of the culprit and its night fighter squadron were left out of the squadron documents. Why was the takeoff time of NT179 left out of the document? Was there a reason? Was it done on purpose so nobody might be able to draw afterward a link between the time NT179 was up in the air and the time frames certain friendly night-fighter pilots were up in the air?

Here are Bill Carp's exact words regarding the Operations Record Book and Combat Report of XXX Sqdn:

> From:Bill Carp
> Date: 11 August 2006, 14:01:28
> Re: Mosquito NT179, Friendly Fire
>
> Hi, Dirk,
>
> According to my research, the XXX Squadron pilot was John Doe. I will be visiting the PRO next week and will see what documents I can find for you.
>
> Cheers
>
> Bill

From: Bill Carp
Date: 12 September 2006 10:59:49
Re: Mosquito NT179

Hi, Dirk,

The mystery deepens!

There is no combat report for John Doe for that night, and no entries in the ORB—but he was responsible. Some units "covered-up" friendly fire incidents, and obviously XXX Squadron was one! Unfortunately, I can't provide more information at present. Sorry.

Cheers

Bill

Please feel free to contact Bill Carp because he checked the combat reports of XXX Sqdn. He has more experience with friendly fire incidents.

Unfortunately, I didn't save the e-mail reply sent by The National Archives pertaining to XXX Sqdn Combat Report photocopies, because it was such a brief answer. It was nonspecific, and the wording was something in the line of, "Photocopies of XXX Sqdn combat reports are unavailable." I didn't bother to write the archivist as to why I couldn't have photocopies of the combat reports for September 28/29, 1944, because I knew Bill Carp was going to check them for me in person.

PS: I wrote Peter Smith a letter, and I'm awaiting his answer.

With my best wishes to you both,

Dirk

November 6, 2006

Dear Jamie and Colin,

Yesterday, November 5, 2006, at around 10:00 a.m., members of BAHAAT visited the crash site in the Koestraat at Neerijse to pinpoint the Rolls-Royce Merlin engine of Mosquito NT179.

The engine's exact location was found quickly with the aid of a metal detector, taking only five minutes, a record time by BAHAAT standards.

So the rumor about the engine never having been salvaged was true.

At first, digging was done by spade. Immediately, small pieces of engine started to come to the surface. Next they struck the Merlin engine itself. The BAHAAT members had brought a small caterpillar-crane, which was just right for this particular occasion.

The earth around the engine was carefully dug away so the Merlin engine could be pulled free.

This done, the engine was tilted in such a position that chains could be wrapped around it.

The chains were fixed to the arm of the small caterpillar-crane, which had just enough power to pull the Rolls-Royce Merlin XXV out of the hole.

The Merlin was then loaded on a trailer together with the loose components found around it.

It was taken to the Belgian village of Erembodegem near the town of Aalst, where it will be cleaned, restored, and put on display in the BAHAAT museum. If all goes according to plan, it will be put on display during the spring of 2007. More importantly, not only the Merlin but also the tragic story behind it will be saved for future generations since BAHAAT gives a central place in their museum to the human history behind the relics found.

Please find attached two photographs of me, taken by a member of BAHAAT.

Dirk

That same day, November 5, 2006, the second engine was also located. It is situated only a few feet away from the first engine, meaning NT179 fell toward earth fairly intact. It was a strange feeling for me standing right in between the two engines because I knew I was standing on the very spot where the cockpit section used to be.

Marc Henckens, the president of BAHAAT, works according to the rules imposed by the Flemish and Belgian authorities. This means he will prepare a full report of his first find (first engine) and address it to the proper authorities before going any further. As you can imagine, it involves a lot of bureaucratic paperwork. Once positive advice is given to Marc and his team, they will excavate the entire plane or what is left of it, so the second engine will probably be salvaged in the near future, if everything goes according to plan.

With my best wishes,

Di

January 19, 2007

Dear Dirk and Colin,

All has been quiet. There have been no new developments. I took advantage of the lull to review our correspondence and came up with several comments, questions, and mixed opinions.

I suggest that, as the next of kin, I request the pertinent information from the National Archives. Dirk, can you provide me with the address?

I will cite the wealth of evidence of Dewar's and Alan's deaths by friendly fire, including the presence of air ministry form 1180 accident card, which lacks identification of the second aircraft, the failure of #21 Squadron to record my brother's time up, and DeHavilland records stating their aircraft NT179 was "shot down by another intruder."

Should we ask for suggestions from Marc Henckens and BAHAAT, Bill Carp, and/or Peter Smith? I'd be willing to write them.

Having served in the RCAF during WWII myself, both in Canada and for a short time in the United Kingdom, I am not unsympathetic to the situation. I'm also aware that the pilot of the other aircraft had a distinguished war record, extending from the Battle of Britain to the end of the war.

So, how far should we push it? Do we have all the information we need now?

With my best wishes for a successful new year for all of us.

Jamie

Dear James,

Here are some suggestions of mine.

1. Regarding the National Archives

I think it would be wise—although expensive—to consider the paid research The National Archives offers, or even better, to hire an independent researcher who knows the holdings of The National Archives, Kew. The National Archives website has a list of several independent researchers. Some of these independent researchers have a website. Consult these websites to compare prices and to know the subjects they specialize in. (Mr. Richard S. Robinson is perhaps the right researcher to help you. See: http://www.na-searcher.co.uk/.)

I'm not able to make the trip to The National Archives myself to do the research—hence the above proposals. There are several private researchers who specialize in RAF matters. I'm but a novice in these matters, as there are many RAF records and forms unknown to me that might eventually shed a brighter light on your questions (e.g., form 1180, the accident card, must have been based on a thorough report. I neither know the name of the report Form 1180 was based on, nor do I know at which archives it is held and whether this report is open to the public yet).

According to Marc Henckens, it may also be worthwhile to check (besides the ORB of 21Sqdn) the ORB of the wing 21 Sqdn belonged to and the ORB of the group it belonged to (No. 2 Group). The same is true for 219 Sqdn.

A hired researcher might also check for the name of your brother's regular navigator.

The Operations Record Book (ORB) holds a form named air ministry form 541, detail of work carried out.

I have sent you a copy of air ministry form 541 for the night of September 28/29, 1944, the one where the takeoff time of NT179 is missing. For each day, a form 541 was prepared, listing the serial numbers of the Mosquitoes that took off that day. Behind each serial number the name of the pilot and his navigator is listed. Checking the ORB of 21 Sqdn for all forms 541 during Dewar's service with 21

Sqdn will give you an idea of the different navigators Dewar crewed with. It will answer your question as to who Dewar's regular navigator was and as to how many operational missions Dewar and Alan ever flew together before the fatal incident. Checking form 541 will confirm or disprove the hearsay about Alan Wiggins not being your brother's regular navigator and about it being their first mission together. It might also shed a light on who Alan's regular pilot was and on what date Alan flew his first operational mission with 21 Sqdn (the latter is also true for Dewar). It should also reveal the Mosquito Dewar was usually assigned to fly. (Did he pilot NT179 for the first time that fatal night?).

Another option is to order copies of all air ministry forms 541 for the period Dewar served with 21 Sqdn.

A third option might be Bill Carp. He visits The National Archives on a regular basis. He might be willing to offer his help in this matter.

2. Regarding Marc Henckens and BAHAAT

I would guess Marc certainly will have some suggestions on how to continue the research. If you won't mind, I will forward your e-mail message to Marc. He will also be able to give you detailed information regarding the engine and the museum.

3. Regarding Bill Carp

Please feel free to contact Brian. As I stated previously, he visits The National Archives on a regular basis. He might be willing to offer his help in this matter because one of the projects he is currently working on is about friendly-fire incidents.

4. Regarding Peter Smith and John Doe

I never received an answer from Peter Smith. Therefore I'd highly appreciate it if you could write him a letter.

It might well be that John Doe still alive today. A person with the name Doe

John (who could be his next of kin) is registered in the New Zealand White Pages. He lives in Port Chalmers, which is close to Dunedin—the town where John Doe was born.

5. Regarding the War Graves Commission

Patience is often a virtue in these matters. I will contact them again, asking them whether my inquiry is treated.

I hope this helps.

Best wishes,

Dirk

Mr Peter Smith

Dear Mr. Smith

My name is Dirk Vander Hulst and I'm writing you from Belgium pertaining to the fate of De Havilland Mosquito NT179 mistaken for a Junkers 88 and shot down by a friendly fighter the night of September 28-29, 1944.

Rumour has it Mosquito NT179 of 21 Squadron was shot down by 219 Squadron Mosquito HK250, flown by Fl Lt John Doe.

Out of an interest for aviation anf local history, I do some research on the unsolved crashes that occurred in my neck of the woodsduring theSecond World War. About four months ago I spoke to an elderly lady, named Mrs. De Keyser, who witnessed the crash of a Mosquito in the field located behind her house. At Neerijse (Belgium). The incident happened in the early hours of 29 September 1944 at about 03.00 AM. The two unfortunates were officially buried near the scene of the crash but were soon after exhumed and transferred to a place unknown to her. Luckily, she had the thoughtfulness to note the names of the two victims. Most amazingly, she kept those names for the next Sixty-two years. Their names were F/O George Dewar MacLeod (RCAF) and F/O Alan Charles Wiggins (RAF), respectively the pilot and navigator of Mosquito NT179.

Unfortunately, there is no Combat Report for Doe that night and no entries in the ORB.

My fellow investigators and I would like to know whether you, as respected researcher can confirm the truth of the Doe rtumour. We'd highly appreciate your advice. We only want the information so we can get closure, not for sny finger-pointing purposes.

I thank you for your help in this matter.

Yours truly,

Dirk vander hulst

Dear Mr. Smith,

I would highly appreciate if you could pass on the following information to John Doe.

Dear Mr. Doe,

I herewith send you the contact information for Flying Officer George Dewar MacLeod's brother and for Flying Officer Alan Charles Wiggins's cousin.

I would like to emphasize that it is not in the least my intention to rip up old sores.

Both families did their grieving long ago and would like to indicate that they are merely searching for information without intending to make any accusations. Dr. James MacLeod, having served in the RCAF himself, both in Canada and the United Kingdom during WWII, is not unsympathetic to the situation. The families of both flying officers are also aware that you had a distinguished war record, extending from the Battle of Britain to the end of the war.

Dr. James MacLeod simply wishes to learn what actually happened to his brother, Dewar, on the night of September 28/29, 1944. James was a bomb aimer in the RCAF and made a short visit to Dewar at his base in Thorney Island. During that visit, Dewar took James for a short flight. That was ten days before Dewar's death. Subsequently, James visited Dewar's squadron again. All they could tell James was that the squadron was performing moon bombing over the Ruhr.

If you do not have any objection against clarifying the circumstances of his brother's death, please feel free to contact Dr. James MacLeod or me. Presently, James is eighty-one years old.

Yours truly,

Dirk Vander Hulst

Dear Madam or Sir,

I'm looking into the fate of Flying Officer MacLeod George Dewar RCAF (J/22008) and Flying Officer Wiggins Alan Charles RAF (153253). Both airmen were with No. 21 (RAF) Squadron. F /O Macleod was my brother.

Both died on September 29, 1944 near Neerijse, Belgium, and are presently buried at Leopoldsburg War Cemetery, Belgium. Do you have detailed information with regard to the different burial locations of the two airmen?

1. For how long were MacLeod and Wiggins buried near the scene of the crash at Neerijse, Belgium (from which date to which date)?

2. Were MacLeod and Wiggins thereupon reburied at Leopoldsburg War Cemetery (Belgium,) or was there an interim reburial at a location unknown to me?

3. Rumor has it MacLeod and Wiggins fell victim to friendly fire. Can you confirm this rumor?

I'm in contact with Colin Wiggins, the nephew of Alan Charles Wiggins. We are eager to learn whether this rumor is true. I thank you in advance for any information you can give me.

Yours sincerely,

James H. Macleod, MD

Dear Mr. MacLeod,

Thank you for your letters dated January 31 and February 8, 2007, seeking some details regarding the death of your brother, Flying Officer George Dewar Macleod RCAF, who sadly lost his life whilst flying with the Royal Air Force during World War II. You have a number of specific queries relating to the loss of your brother that I will endeavor to answer.

You wish to know for how long your brother and his navigator, F/O Wiggins, were buried near the scene of the crash of their aircraft at Neerijse, Belgium. The burial form forwarded by No. 250 Coy RASC, who were responsible for the burial of your brother and F/O Wiggins, is dated September 29, 1944, the date of the crash. The exact date of reburial is not given in any of the documents we have relating to the loss of your brother. There are two reburial slips dated December 23, 1946, but whether this date is just when these were completed or when your brother was reburied I cannot tell.

I am unable to advise you from the information that is available whether your brother and F/O Wiggins were reburied prior to being laid to rest in the Leopoldsburg War Cemetery. It is possible that the CWGC may be able to help you with this point.

There is nothing in our records that corroborate the rumor that Mosquito NT179 fell victim to friendly fire. In fact, the following information is given:

> At 2:45 a.m. on September, 29, 1944, an aircraft crashed at Wolfhaejen, near Neeryssche, and was later identified as a Mosquito. Witnesses stated that it had been pursued by a German night fighter.

I hope the above information may be of some assistance.

Yours sincerely,

Mrs. S. A. Dickinson
ADBS (RAF)

Dear Dirk and Colin,

Surprise! Surprise! Nine months after I'd requested them, Canada Archives disgorged its documents—as long as a full-term pregnancy.

But what a gestation! The full minutes of a court of inquiry held in October 1944 and attended by then FL Doe . . . and more quotes from those mysterious "witnesses," including Father Robeyns (the only one identified) describing that mysterious German aircraft with its guns blazing.

With my best wishes,

Jamie

March 4, 2007

Dear Sir:

Re: J-22008. George Dewar MACLEOD
Our Reference—Notre reference
Q-06/07-i-44t22

In reply to your letter of August 24, 2006, concerning the above named, I am pleased to enclose copies of relevant documents from his military service records, which I hope will be of interest to you.

I regret that the large number of inquiries received in our section has led to delays in our response time.

Sincerely,

Gregg J. McCooeye
Analyst, ATIP and Personnel Records Division
Services Branch
Encl.

PROCEEDINGS OF COURT OF INQUIRY
OR INVESTIGATION

FLYING ACCIDENT

COMPOSITION OF THE COURT (OR NAME OF INVESTIGATING OFFICER)

LIST OF WITNESSES

FINDINGS OF THE COURT OR INVESTIGATING OFFICER

3. The purpose of and instructions for the flight(s) were as follows :

Aircraft Type and Number	(i) Who ordered the flight? (ii) For what purpose, (iii) Special instructions of work, (iv) How ma... date the pilot? (v, by whom?
	(i) To 2 fly any
	(ii) Operations
	(iii) Nil
	(iv) No

4. The aircraft took off as follows :

Aircraft Type and Number	Time	Place from which	Weather conditions including strength and direction of surface wind, at the time and place of take-off
Hampden VI NT 179	2359	Thornaby Island	Irrelevant

5. The accidents occurred at the place and on the date set forth on the front page of this Form. Further details are as follows :

Time	Exact location of each, including height (if) where relevant	Weather conditions including strength and direction of surface wind, condition of light, etc.) at the time and place of accident
0044	UPPERDALES	10/10 Cloud 8000 feet, hazy, visibility poor, Moon just setting.

6. The flying experience of the pilot prior to this flight was :

PILOT(S) (a)	Hours flown (quote to nearest hour)											
		Within 6 months prior to accident					Total solo (Dual and Single)		Total solo (Single) (d)			
Name, Age, when trained on type named	Type of aircraft including your own type (c)	Day and Night		Night (i)		On type named	On types opposed	On type named	On types opposed			
		Dual	Total	Dual	Total							
				I R R E L E V A N T.								

7 (i) have examined the following aircraft, engine, flight authorization book, and pilot's flying log books and also Form 700 and have ascertained :

Description of book and form	Remarks, including reasons how supplementary or conforming actions of estimates and entries at necessary inspections were carried out prior to the flight.
	Above mentioned books and forms not considered relevant.

NOTE.—If any of these Documents have not been examined, this must be stated and reason given.

8. We (i) ~~have~~ ~~have not~~ visited the scene of the accident ~~before~~ aircraft ~~was~~ were removed and have found the following material facts :

9. We (i) have been unable to obtain the evidence of the following material witnesses :

Name	Rank	Unit	Reason preventing obtaining of evidence	Have appeared with evidence
G. D. McLeod	P/O	21 Sqdn	Death	Victim
A. C. Wiggins	F/O	21 Sqdn	Death	Victim

10 CONCLUSIONS. Under this Heading the following should always be included :

    (a) Brief description of the accident and its attendant circumstances.
    (b) Diagnosis of cause or causes including all contributory factors.
    (c) Recommendations, if called for by the convening authority.

(A) A Mosquito light bomber which was returning from Operations inside Germany, approached Brussels in such a way that it was regarded with suspicion. A controlled interception against this aircraft was successful; the crew of the night fighter mistook the Mosquito for a JU.88 and shot it down.

(B) The following circumstances led to the accident:
    (i) The No 2 Group aircraft returning from Germany did so on a track and at a height about which there were no friendly movement warnings at the time in question. Although it is admitted that such action may be operationally unavoidable it nevertheless led to the pilot being given an 'X' designation and an interception attempted.
    (ii) By coincidence a night fighter under control of the same G.C.I. had previously that night shot down an a/c which had behaved in a very similar way.
    (iii) The No 2 Group aircraft was not showing I.F.F. Type 'V' and 'Resin' lights were either not showing or not fitted.
    (iv) The G.C.I. Controller told the pilot of the night fighter that he thought the 'Bogey' was a 'Bandit'. Later when the pilot requested help as to identification he was out of effective G.C.I. range and none could be given.
    (v) Visibility was such that the pilot recognised his target as a JU.88 and was not aware of his mistake until, by the light of the flames, he saw the Allied stripes. Night glasses were not being carried.

(C) We do not consider that anyone concerned in this accident was guilty of culpable negligence. Whether avoidable or not the light bomber behaved in a similar way to an a/c and the defence organisation was therefore justified in initiating action. Absence of any artificial means of identification left the crew of the night fighter with the responsibility of recognition. We are satisfied that they took every

C O P Y

Fr : M.R. & E. Service, R.A.F., PARIS.

To: Air Ministry (P.4 Cas), 77, Oxford Street, W.1

Date: 29th March, 1945.

Ref : MRES/S.20%/1.

CASUALTY ENQUIRY NO.17

J.22008 - P/O. G.D. McLeod - Pilot.
153243 - P/O. A.C. Wiggins- Navigator.

Father D.E. Robeyns was interviewed at Louvain in connection
with the crash.

He stated that at 2.45 am. on the 29th Sept. 1944, an aircraft
crashed in flames at Wolfhagen, near Neeryssche, and was later
identified as a Mosquito.   Witnesses stated that it had been pursued
by a German night fighter and had exploded in the air just before
crashing.   Bits of two bodies were found about 100 yards apart and
approximately 150 yards from the remnants of the plane.

The two airmen were buried in a common grave in a field near
the scene of the crash.   A British Padre and 21 Belgian soldiers
officiated at the funeral.   The Padre's name was given as follows:-

                    Rev. H.D. Stapley,
                    Nesta, 1, Lynch Crescent,
                    Winscombe, Somerset,

Father Robeyns was quite positive of the identification of the
two men.   This information has been given to G.R. & E. who will
remove the bodies to a Cemetery and notify you through the usual
channels.

                    SGD. ? Shaw, F/L.
                for Squadron Leader, Officer i/c,
                    M.R. & E.S., R.A.F., PARIS.

Copy to A.D.C.R. & E.

CANADIAN CASUALTY BRANCH

73-77 Oxford Street, XXXXXXXXXXXXXXXXXX
XXXXXXXXXXXX
London, W.1, England, 27th April, 1945.

The Secretary,
Dept. of National Defence for Air,
Rieger Building,
Ottawa, Ontario,
C A N A D A.

ATTENTION : R.O.A.

Can/J22008 F/O S.B.McLEOD

1. Reference my message R.079 dated 13th February, 1945,
it is advised that M.R.A.F. Service, Paris, have now replied to
our enquiries regarding the burial place for the above noted
officer.

2. The reply states that Father D.X.Mobeyns was interviewed at
Louvain and he stated "at 2.45 a.m. on the 29th September, 1944, an
aircraft crashed in flames at Wolfsweijen near Kerrysaghs and was
later identified as a Mosquito. Witnesses stated that it had been
pursued by a German night fighter and had exploded in the air just
before crashing. Bits of two bodies were found about 100 yards
apart and approximately 150 yards from the remnants of the plane.

3. F/O McLeod and F/O Siggins (not R.C.A.F.) were buried in a
common grave in a field near the scene of the crash. A British
Padre and 21 Belgian soldiers officiated at the funeral. The
Padre's name was given as follows :-

                    Reverend N.L.Stapley,
                        North,
                            1 Lynch Crescent,
                                Winscombe, Somerset.

4. This information has been given to the appropriate Graves
Registration authorities who will remove the bodies to a Cemetery
and notify this Branch of further burial details. These details
will be passed to you when this action has been taken.

                    (J.G.Martin) Wing Commander,
                    for Air Officer Commanding-in-Chief,
                    R.C.A.F.Overseas.

AJM/GB/KJA

Dear Mr. Vander Hulst,

First, I must apologies for the long delay in getting any information to you regarding your letter to Mr. Peter Smith dated October 30, 2006. I was not aware of that letter until he passed it on to me in late February this year and said that he had advised you he had done so. I was still considering what action to take when he told me he had received an e-mail from you addressed to me and would print it out and send it on. However this arrived only two days ago

Yes, I was the person responsible for the shooting down of the Mosquito in 1944.

After all these years, I am somewhat hazy as to where and what I was doing at the time in question, as my log books, which would have helped, covering my flying career up to the 1950s were lost many years ago, after my return to New Zealand.

Your letter has clarified the date and the squadron I was with at the time. I now remember I was supernumerary Sqdn/Ldr, not FWt, on 219 Squadron, pending posting to a command position elsewhere, but I cannot remember the name of my radar operator at that time.

I have no need to tell you that your letter reopened the horror of the moment when we realized we had made a ghastly mistake, in that the target aircraft was a Mosquito and not a JU 88, which we both believed it to be. I recall it was a very dark night, and we were on patrol somewhere over Holland. Our ground control radar unit informed us that they had a target for us, and following their instructions, we eventually made radar contact and closed in for a visual. We both believed the aircraft to be a JU 88. I then opened fire, just one short burst, and the aircraft caught fire. It dived away immediately, and we saw in the light of the flames that it was a Mosquito. We watched it go down, hoping against hope that the crew would bail out, and then we saw the aircraft crash in flames. I told our ground control people there and then what had happened and shortly after returned to base.

I do not understand why there was no combat report or entries in the ORB because apart from informing ground control at the time of the action, on landing we filled out the required combat report with the duty intelligence officer, giving all details. I remember I was very worried at the time, believing that there would be an inquiry and I would be in serious trouble. However, as I recall it, nothing ever came of it, and soon after I was posted for duty with No. 488 NZ Sqdn. finishing the war operating from stations in France and Holland.

I was never aware of the identities of the crew of the Mosquito or the Sqdn involved, but now with that knowledge, this matter takes a much more personal aspect. Over the years it troubled me from time to time, but I am afraid I never did anything about it, and I suppose the passage of time eased my conscience. As far as I know, no one other than service personnel of that period knew anything about this matter until now. Certainly not my family; it was not the sort of thing that one talked about. I have never been great on correspondence and have found this letter very difficult to write.

What can I say after all these years except that I am so very sorry that my action in 1944 resulted in the deaths of those two young men and undoubtedly caused a lot of anguish and grief to their families and friends?

I cannot think of anything else to add, but you now have my address, and I will be only too willing to help if anything further is needed to close out this tragic affair,

Yours sincerely,

John Doe

March 19, 2007

Dear Dirk and Colin,

Congratulations, Dirk. Your persistence has been rewarded. Congratulations to you too, Colin, on our success and on that beautiful big red BINGO!

The best to you both,

Jamie

Mr. John Doe,

This concerns the communication you received recently from Dirk Vander Hulst and your reply.

I am the younger brother of the pilot, F/O George Dewar MacLeod.

I appreciate your open and honest response, and I want you to know that I bear no animosity toward you. We're all well aware of your distinguished wartime record.

Since I too was a member of the RCAF, I'm aware of how easily friendly fire can occur. and I've heard of a few cases of failure to activate the IFF. I understand that such the case in this instance.

As Dirk has told you, we only want information for closure (that overworked word), and we (Dirk, the navigator's next of kin, and I) are all agreed to let the matter drop.

We apologize for bringing back those memories. We wish you well and consider the case closed.

Sincerely yours,

James MacLeod

May 15, 2007

Dear Dr MacLeod,

Thank you for your letter, which I have just read, having been away from home the last three weeks. I very much appreciate what you have to say, and what a relief it has been to me to realize now that everything can be put to rest. I have already had similar letters from family members of the other airman concerned, FO Wiggins, and can only say thank you for the understanding way you and everyone else have dealt with this matter and express again my sorrow that the event ever happened in the first place.

Thank you again for what you have written. It is difficult to express my relief knowing that now that the whole matter is, as you say, "case closed."

Yours sincerely,

John Doe

What follows is A Potpourri—

The Mosquito Aircraft

Foreword to "Friendly Fire"

Excerpt of "Friendly Fire"

Our Dad

Dewar

Followed by a trip to Belgium, to Rosa's home in Neerijse and the crash site, to the Broken Wing Museum and the engine and the Leopoldsburg Military Cemetery.

THE MOSQUITO AIRCRAFT

"The Mosquito . . . makes me furious. I turn green and yellow with envy!"

—Reichsmarshall Hermann Goering, Commander Luftwaffe, 1943

Goering was due to address a parade in Berlin on January 30, 1943, to observe the tenth anniversary of the Nazis being voted into power. Three Mosquitoes launched a low-level attack on the main Berlin broadcasting station, keeping Goering off the air. The Reichsmarshall was not amused.

The Mosquito was the outcome of a revolutionary concept: that a bomber would be much faster if it had only a wooden fuselage, with no guns and no gunners, and so was free of the structure and fuel load needed to carry them. Materials and construction were far cheaper than conventional aircraft, requiring fewer skilled workers, and production time was far shorter than for metal aircraft.

Sheets of laminated plywood were formed to the desired shape in large concrete moulds, each holding one half of the fuselage, split vertically.

Once all the wiring and control systems were in place, the two halves were joined by a specially prepared glue, reinforced by many screws.

The completed fuselage was lowered onto the previously prepared wing (a single unit of plywood and fastened by more glue and more screws).

Screws

Powered by Rolls-Royce Merlin engines, it was faster than any other aircraft, Allied or enemy, and remained so until the advent of the German jet plane 262. Once the plane was put into operation, it became apparent that it could be equipped with cannon or rockets and two five hundred—pound bombs and still outrun any enemy fighter.

It was extremely versatile as a day or night fighter, fighter-bomber (Dewar's), photo reconnaissance, and pathfinder squadron marker.

In contrast to strategic long-distance air attacks, tactical air force operations were conducted in support of ground troops. The Second Tactical Air Force (2nd TAF) attacked trains, rail lines, marshaling yards, and flying bomb and rocket launch platforms. The night fighters and fighter-bombers were particularly suited to this type of warfare, as well as an occasional attack on various Gestapo headquarters to free prisoners.

Allied air supremacy in general prevented enemy movements during daylight. At night, the Mosquito was supreme, and it soon became noted for low-level precision bombing. (On one occasion, Dewar arrived back from a flight with two hundred feet of telephone wire trailing from his wings.)

Dirk Vander Hulst also published an account of our findings, an excerpt of which is presented here. He was kind enough to ask me to provide the foreword.

FOREWORD

JAMES MACLEOD

Sixty-two years after my older brother, Dewar, was killed in action, I learned, through Dirk Vander Hulst that he had been killed by friendly fire.

The term friendly fire refers to fire coming from allied forces as opposed to that coming from enemy forces. It is as old as warfare itself.

The incidence of friendly fire is reported in wildly varying numbers, depending on the source. According to one reliable report, it accounted for less than 2 percent of casualties in World War II, the Korean War, and the Vietnam War, rising to about 15 percent in the Persian Gulf War.[3]

Most incidents are categorized, in decreasing order of frequency:

- ground-to-ground; for example, artillery fire striking allied infantry
- air-to-ground, such as aircraft strafing or bombing its own troops
- ground-to-air incidents, such as allied planes shot down by antiaircraft fire
- air-to-air, in which one allied aircraft shoots down another allied plane

The event described here falls into the last category—air to air—and involved my brother, George Dewar MacLeod, and his navigator, Alan Charles Wiggins.

Today the media are quick to seize on episodes of friendly fire. Massive public attention may be focused on any incident, frequently with zero tolerance for error.[4] They are quick to

---

[3]   Eric Schmitt, "ARTICLE NAME," *New York Times*. Aug. 10, 1991, PAGE NUMBER(S).

[4]   Bryan, C.D.B. *Friendly Fire*. (New York: Bantam Books, 1976).

fault the offending crew, and some allude to a military hush up. In World War II, friendly fire was known to occur, but it wasn't publicized.[5]

Of course the pilots feel badly. To quote a combat stress expert, "Friendly fire is perhaps the greatest horror and fear of war. To know you have killed a buddy, a countryman or an ally is a massive psychological *horror.*"[6]

And that word—horror—recurs again and again in reports. In the case reported here the pilot, in describing his initial reaction on realizing he had shot down a fellow allied aircraft, speaks of "the *horror* of the moment."

More recently, the death of a British soldier in Iraq from aircraft fire led to much media abuse, until the BBC's correspondent stated, "It was obvious from the cockpit video that the pilots were appalled by their mistake. They are not just remorseful, they are weeping. They are beside themselves."[7] "These guys live in hell for the balance of their lives."[8]

Furthermore, punishment may well cause soldiers to hold their fire in later situations in which they should not.

Veterans and those still serving know friendly fire for what it is: an inevitable part of the confusion of warfare. Its frequency can be lessened by technology and especially by training, but it can never be eliminated.

In our case, we were never informed of the friendly fire. But there was a court of inquiry, whose report is in the Canadian National Archives.[9] The loss to friendly fire was also recorded by the plane's manufacturer, DeHavilland,[10] which keeps track of all its aircraft and whose files are available to anyone on the Internet.

---

[5] Caddick-Adams, Peter, military historian.

[6] Joseph Mancusi, combat stress expert, quoted by Finlo Rohrer, *BBC News Magazine*, March 20, 2007.

[7] BBC News. 6 Feb 2007. Friendly Fire footage revealed. Paul Wood.

[8] BBC News. 6 Feb 2007. Friendly Fire footage revealed. Ward Carroll (former Navy pilot, now editor of website Militsry.Com).

[9] Canadian National Archives, Ottawa Canada.

[10] Online: http://www.dehavilland.ukf.net/mosquito.htm.

It was a bit of a shock for me to learn of the friendly fire factor from Dirk some sixty-odd years after the event, but as I told Dirk, we did our mourning at the time of Dewar's death.

Should families be informed of the manner of death? I'm certainly glad our parents never learned of it; it would only have compounded their grief. Colin Wiggins, nephew of the navigator, Alan Wiggins, says, "I thank God that Alan's mother never learned what actually happened."

According to the Pentagon, many families don't want to know.[11]

---

[11] Pentagon via *NYT.* 2/14/91

FRIENDLY FIRE

BY DIRK VANDER HULST

Thorney Island, September 28/29, 1944

No. 21 Squadron operated from an airfield on Thorney Island, a peninsula on the southern coast of England, near Portsmouth. Together with its sister units, 464 RAAF and 487 RNZAF squadrons, the three comprised 140 Wing of the Second Tactical Air Force. The RAF's Second Tactical Air Force was a specialist air force that was formed specifically to support the British/Canadian ground forces in the field. The main job of No. 21 Squadron, at least in this stage of the war, was to stop any enemy transport—road, rail, or river—from bringing supplies to the front. They patrolled in their quick and nimble Mosquitoes behind the front lines, usually by moonlight. This was also the case on the night of September 28-29, 1944, when the crews of 21 Squadron were briefed on the railways Rheine-Munster-Hannum and a small area east of the battle line. In other words, a railway patrol was set for that night. The Mosquito or "Mossie" was perfect for this job.

The squadron was equipped with the de Havilland Mosquito Mark VI, a twin-engine fighter-bomber made entirely of plywood. The nose combination of four 0.303-inch (7.7mm) machine guns that fired at a rate of one thousand rounds per minute and four 20mm cannons at a rate of six hundred rounds per minute gave the Mosquito Mk VI a very nasty sting. Mixed in with the ammunition were rounds of high explosives, tracers, and incendiaries, so when they fired the tracers could be clearly seen. In addition, it could carry four five hundred—pound (227kg) bombs. Sometimes on a really dark night, two one million candlepower parachute flares were substituted for two bombs, which enabled the crew to illuminate the target before bombing.

On that fatal September night, twelve Mosquitos of No. 21 Squadron took off at intervals of a quarter of an hour, sometimes a half hour, to harass transports in the designated patrol area for as long as possible (on average for a period up to six hours). The first Mosquito had already left Thorney Island at 8:15 p.m. The very last Mossie took off at exactly one minute before midnight. This last plane bore aircraft serial number NT179; sitting in the cockpit was the Canadian pilot MacLeod with the British navigator Wiggins at his side. This was only the second op they had flown together. F/O Wiggins was probably a temporary replacement for F/O Miller, MacLeod's regular navigator. It was to be MacLeod's thirteenth operational mission and Wiggins's seventh.

It was on the way back from Germany that fate turned against the new team; it was then that their aircraft was detected and regarded with suspicion by a ground control interception radar unit of the RAF set up somewhere in liberated territory. Mosquito NT179 was not transmitting IFF—Identification, Friend or Foe—and so GCI was unable to determine whether this was a friendly or enemy plane. In addition, NT179 approached Brussels on a track and at a height about which there were no friendly movement warnings at the time in question. In other words, for the GCI controller, NT179 was an unidentified and potentially enemy plane, in air force jargon a "bogey." Therefore, the GCI unit decided to proceed to interception and vectored one of its Mosquito night fighters to an interception point to make visual contact and check whether this bogey was a bandit (an enemy plane), because by coincidence a night fighter under control of that same GCI unit had previously that night shot down an enemy aircraft that had behaved in a very similar way.

The GCI controller directed the Mosquito night fighter crew, consisting of a pilot and an airborne radar operator/navigator, to a point to the rear of the bogey. Once the airborne radar operator, seated next to the pilot, made contact with the suspect aircraft on his radar set, he directed the pilot to a location where visual contact could be made, at which point the pilot took over.

Sixty-two years later, thanks to the help of two foreign researcher-writers, I traced the night fighter pilot who had intercepted Mosquito NT179 and shot it down by mistake. The man, by now almost ninety years old, wrote me an open and honest letter and had no objection to my publishing his account here:

> Yes, I was the person responsible for the shooting down of the Mosquito in 1944. I have no need to tell you that your letter reopened the horror of the moment when we realized we had made a ghastly mistake, in that the target aircraft was a Mosquito and not a JU 88, which we both believed it to be. I recall it was a very dark night, and we were on patrol somewhere over Holland. Our ground control radar unit informed us that they

had a target for us, and following their instructions, we eventually made radar contact and closed in for a visual. We both believed the aircraft to be a JU 88. I then opened fire, just one short burst, and the aircraft caught fire. It dived away immediately, and we saw in the light of the flames that it was a Mosquito. We watched it go down, hoping against hope that the crew would bail out, and then we saw the aircraft crash in flames. I told our ground control people there and then what had happened, and shortly after returned to base.

MacLeod and Wiggins were shot down over Neerijse at 2:44 a.m. Visibility was such (weather conditions: 10/10 cloud, 8,000 feet, hazy, visibility poor, the moon just setting) that the pilot mistook his target as a Junkers 88 and was not aware of his mistake until, by the light of the flames, he saw the Allied stripes. In addition, the night fighter crew had not seen any resin lights when closing in from behind. These were small lights for air-to-air identification by night. They were either not showing or not fitted onto NT179. It should also be noted that the GCI controller told the night fighter pilot that he thought the bogey was a bandit. Later when the pilot requested help as to the identification, he was out of effective GCI range and none could be given.

Be that as it may, as a rule IFF sets and resin lights were both switched for specified distances departing and approaching Allied-held territory. These means of identification betrayed aircraft and contributed to Allied losses when left switched on, especially so as to IFF sets, because the Germans took bearings of any signals emanating from enemy aircraft.

OUR DAD

In 1915, a new battalion was being formed in Nova Scotia: the eighty-fifth Canadian Infantry Battalion (Nova Scotia Highlanders). It immediately became known familiarly as "the eighty-fifth."

George MacLeod left his father's home in Strathlorne, Cape Breton, and was one of the first to enlist. He did so as a private and progressed through the ranks over the next three years—as a corporal, then as a sergeant, and then a company sergeant-major, and he finished as a lieutenant.

Strathlorne, Cape Breton.

Private MacLeod.

Lieut. MacLeod.

The troops trained together in Nova Scotia and in England. Then they proceeded to France, where they were involved in several battles, including Vimy Ridge and Passchendaele.

They trained together, fought together, and many of them died together; the survivors remained loyal to the eighty-fifth for the rest of their lives.

They were the first allied unit to enter the city of Louvain, Belgium, after the Armistice.

Burgomaster and Council of Louvain with 85th Officers

In another generation, in another war, George's son would crash to his death only five miles away.

Before going overseas, while at an ice rink in Halifax, George stepped out on to the ice in skates and promptly fell. A pretty girl laughed at him.

She was slim and trim (and remained so all her life). Her name was Marion Hall, and she was the sheriff's daughter.

They were married before he went overseas.

George and Marion, 1920

After the war, George attended all the eighty-fifth meetings and visited the veterans' hospital regularly. He attended the outdoor Remembrance Day service, taking us with him. He regularly bought us each a poppy every year.

He took a job as a Ford salesman and remained with the same company until his death. As the years passed, he developed a growing reputation for honesty and fair dealing and consequently, a growing and loyal clientele. My friends often quoted their parents to me: "You'll always get a fair deal from George MacLeod."

Dewar and I loved and respected our father, and we never lost that respect. Beneath a great deal of teasing, there was a great amount of love. He lived for his children, and we knew it.

He was always there for us—school functions, sports, any occasions (in the background). After we enlisted, first Dewar and then me, he was always at the train station when we came home on leave.

Even wartime restrictions couldn't stop him. When I went overseas, we were taken on a nonstop troop train from Montreal through to Halifax, where we stopped only when we were inside a restricted, fenced-in area at the waterfront. When I got off the train, there Dad was. He'd wangled his way in. (He had done so for Dewar's departure, I learned from Dewar subsequently.)

After Dewar was killed, I came home on compassionate leave. The Halifax train station was crowded as usual. Dad was always at the gate, but this time he wasn't there! I was bewildered. Dad was never sick, and certainly not so sick that he couldn't meet me. *He was always there!* A family friend met me and drove me home.

After I saw Mom, I visited a short time with her and then went upstairs. Dad was in bed but awake, and he knew me. We even discussed my future (he brought it up) and that I would go to college.

His condition deteriorated progressively. Within two days, we had to take him to the hospital, where, five days after my return and three months after Dewar's death, he died of cerebral thrombosis—a stroke—at age fifty-three.

The funeral was held in our home and was crowded. When I came out of the house to walk to the cemetery, a few blocks away, the street was crowded with strange middle-aged men. I realized they were the men of the eighty-fifth paying their last respects. They would walk to the cemetery too.

Excerpt of letter from J. L. Ralston
Commanding Officer, 85th Battalion, WWI
Minister of Defense, Government of Canada, WWII

J. L. Ralston, Ottawa
January 16, 1945.

Dear Mrs. McLeod:

I have just received the very, very sad news of the passing of my dear friend and comrade, George McLeod. This blow, following as it does the grievous loss of your boy, is a tragedy of war which I know must be well nigh unbearable.

I recall his unswerving devotion to duty and his selfless loyalty, and the pride he had in the eighty-fifth, and I am deeply grateful for having had the privilege of his friendship. He was a fine soldier. Many times he faced not only the enemy but death itself, in the line, and I cannot help feeling that in the loss of your boy, the ordeal was more poignant than even those he had gone through in the Great War, and his heart was broken.

With my warmest regards and my sincere sympathy to you and your son.

Yours very truly,

(Sgd) J. L. Ralston

"He was a devout man, patriotic . . . awed by God and King as only those born before the war could be. He followed the rules laid down by parent, schoolmaster, officer and Bible; He was steadfast, polite and unquestioning and he never did less than whatever he was expected to do."

—The Englishman's Daughter, Ben MacIntyre[12]

I encountered this in my casual reading. Although it referred to the typical English soldier, my immediate reaction was, "That's my dad!"

Within a period of four months, our family had been reduced from four to two—my mother and me. She lived for another twenty years.

I finished the war behind a desk at RCAF headquarters in Halifax. Then I attended Dalhousie University Medical School, took further training in surgery, and practiced surgery in Liverpool, NS, Halifax, and California.

---

[12] The Englishman's Daughter, Ben MacIntyre., New York, New York, Farrar, Straus & Giroux, 2003, Page 103.

Dewar

Dewar got off to a good start. At the time of his enlistment, the recruiting office commented, "Exceptional qualifications. Outstanding in appearance and very clever."

He was undoubtedly a good pilot. During his training at EFTS, his flying was rated second only to that of a remustered ground crew officer with previous flying experience. At SFTS, he was number one.

During all those evaluations, as well as those as a flying instructor, his flying was rated as average only once. One examiner not only rated him above average but actually included the word *careful* in his summation.

Our investigations were totally successful, with one exception. We failed to determine not only why their IFF was not on but why, to quote the court of investigation, their aircraft was "on a track and at a height about which there were no friendly movement warnings at the time in question."

OUR BELGIAN TRIP

(With my son Dewar as photographer)
April 21-22, 2007

NEERIJSE

Rosa at home with her husband. She's imitating the sound of the aircraft as it descended.

Leaving her house and walking up the Koestraat.
(The plane came down just beyond it, on the right of the road; the bodies were thrown to the left.)

Pointing to the cornfield (the crash site).

Through the fence

Pointing to the temporary burial site with Dirk.

temporary burial site

The temporary burial site

BROKEN WINGS MUSEUM

February 6, 2007

Dear Mr. Macleod,

Dear Mr. Wiggins,

Your address was given to me by our common friend, Dirk Vander Hulst, because we have a mutual interest in the air war over Belgium. Allow me to introduce myself and the organizations I represent.

For about twenty years, I have been studying the air war over our country. This resulted in the publication of several books and articles, including magazines like *FlyPast*, etc. With several friends, we've been gathering information from archives (Public Records Office, Bundesarchiv de Deck, American Archives Washington DC). We can say that our files of incidents (crashes, air combats, bombings) during the occupation of Belgium (May 10 1940 till September 1944) give more or less a complete view of what happened here, as the Germans were very good in recording what happened in the territories they were occupying, and we've been able to track down these documents, on which we could built further with Allied sources.

Studying the air war after the September '44 is much more difficult. There are no such documents made up by the British and Americans, so we have to search for pieces like a jigsaw puzzle all over the world. For example, we have the list of all the Commonwealth burials in Belgium and are able to identify the crews, serials, etc., but not always the exact location as to where crews lost their lives.

On such moments, local historians like Dirk play a major role in our investigation. Although we've been trying to help him as much as possible, it is thanks to the painstaking research of Dirk that after sixty years, we all know more about a very sad incident, in which your brothers were involved. We are all very grateful to him, and to you, for sharing all the info we have now.

Back in 1996, we established the Belgian Aviation History Association, which has almost three hundred members now, all people who are interested in this subject (both military as civil, WWI & WWI, etc. Also see www.baha.be). Since I was a cofounder, I am the vice president of BAHA. Within BAHA, an independent group was formed, called the BAHA Archaeology Team (BAHAAT). This unit mainly searches for remains of WWII planes in Belgium, both above and under the earth surface. See www.bahaat.be for more details. Rather than old documents (which we also collect), we think that one can more see and feel the stories by displaying real artifacts, dug up from the mud. Therefore, we established our own museum called Broken Wings, which is open every Sunday afternoon during the spring and summer. (It is open again on March 25.)

All through the past ten years, we've gathered a lot of interest in the media (local and national TV, but also CNN). We do not receive any financial help. All our operations (hiring cranes, transport) and the operation of our museum (rent, electricity) is paid for by the BAHAAT members.

Now for our future plans. You know that a few months ago, thanks to the local investigations of Dirk, we were able to dig up one engine of your brother's Mosquito. Since this artifact was lying just beneath the surface, it is damaged by corrosion. We were also able to trace engine number two. We did not excavate this one because local regulations are rather unclear. We are discussing all this with the archaeological council of Flanders, asking for clear instructions on how we should work.

We've cleaned the Rolls Royce engine as well as we could to have it displayed in our museum by the start of the new season (March 25). To show the authorities and the official archaeological council, we are always happy to participate in all kinds of national events in which heritage is in the focus. Therefore, the Flemish government (Belgium is a federal state, which does not makes things easier for us) organizes "Erfgoeddag," "Heritage Day." They invite local and national organizations who are active in these matters, to show the public what they do. And because we feel that we are participating in sharing one aspect of heritage with the general public, our museum, Broken Wings, was once again this year accepted as a partner (along with several hundreds of heritage initiatives in our country). Every year they choose a certain theme, in which the participants have to fit, and this year they suggested "the values of heritage" (whatever that may mean . . .). So I proposed to them that in our museum, we should show a part of our history of which very little is known, and one that one can make parallels with what is happening today in the world. Since the sad incident of the downing of the Mosquito is a case of friendly fire, we thought that it would be interesting to let people know that what is happening today in battle zones like Afghanistan and Iraq happened as well over our country sixty years ago. We hope to have the engine displayed among our other artifacts, with some pictures, a scale model, and some informative texts.

BAHAAT is also working on a documentary, called *Vijandslucht, "Enemy Skies."* With this film, we are trying to show how the air war over Belgium was fought, illustrated with our activities over the past ten years (digging up Allied and Axis artifacts, with wartime archive material, etc.). In our team, we have a professional cameraman who works for the Belgian TV and who films during our operations. He was also there during the recovery of the engine, and this incident will also be in the film. This film, spoken in Dutch, will be showed for the first time on April 8 in our museum but will also be shown during Heritage Day on April 22.

Of course, you are most welcome to join us in one of these events. Just let us know. We are all looking forward hearing from you!

Yours most sincerely,

Cynrik de Decker

THE ENGINE AND PLAQUE (IN FLEMISH)

Rolls Royce Merlin XXV
afkomstig van Mosquito Mk VI NT179 (21 Squadron)

Deze machine werd op 29 september 1944 het slachtoffer van "Friendly Fire", de NT179 werd per vergissing neergehaald door een andere Mosquito. De Flying Officers George D. Macleod (RCAF - foto rechts) en Alan C. Wiggins (RAF - foto links) kwamen om het leven te Neerijse. De identiteit van deze machine kwam in 2006 aan het licht daar een van de ooggetuigen, Rosa De Keyser, na de crash een pasfotootje vond van een van de slachtoffers, en zich hun namen nog herinnerde.
Lokale historicus Dirk Van der Hulst onderzocht het hele incident verder. Na zestig jaar liet de Mosquito-vliegenier die de NT179 neerhaalde van zich horen. Hij was een erg ervaren piloot die door de grondradar op een verkeerd spoor werd gezet.
De motor werd op 5 november 2006 tijdens een prospectie door BAHAAT bovengehaald. Daar de Merlin erg ondiep stak, is er zware corrosie.

© Arqoli 2007

Dirk and his father translating the plaque for me.

Being interviewed by Cynric
de Decker, VP of BAHAA.

Sharing a chuckle with Cynric.

Being presented with a portion of Dewar's engine (supercharger impeller).

With Cynrik and my son, George Dewar MacLeod II

Sender :
Olivier Arquin
Panoramalaan 13
B-1500 Halle
Belgium
Phone : 0032/473/30 10 35

Dr. James MacLeod
706 North Hillcrest Road,
Beverley Hills, California, 90210-3517
U.S.A.

Brussels, May 23rd 2007

Dear Mister MacLeod

We where very pleased and honored to welcome you and Dirk Vander Hulst in our Broken Wings museum on Saturday, April 21st 2007 at Erembodegem, Belgium.

With this letter we would like to thank you again for your presence, which meant a lot and was most appreciated by all members of the Belgian Aviation History Association's Archeology Team!

You'll also find a disk in this envelope including all the pictures taken during your visit at the museum.

God bless you and your family!

Yours truly

Cynrik De Decker	Paul Callebaut	Stefan Delannoit
Hans Asselman	Ulrik De Neve	Dirk De Quick
Wim De Quick	Marnick De Tant	Wim Govaerts
Herwin Heyman	Sven Petterson	Dany Saey
Maurits Saey	Chris Van Heghe	Ludo Van Hout
Luc Van Lierde	Koen Vantorre	Eric Vormezeele
Karl Debulpaep	Jean-Pierre Hodgson	Tom D'Hoker
Olivier Arquin		

Leuvestraat 4b – 9320 Erembodegem
Belgium

Leopoldsburg British Military Cemetery

FLYING OFFICER
G.D. MACLEOD
PILOT
ROYAL CANADIAN AIR FORCE
29TH SEPTEMBER 1944 AGE 23

ACKNOWLEDGEMENTS

Acknowledgements must go first to Dirk Vander Hulst. He investigated the rumor of a world war II aircraft crash in the area, found the site. above all, he found Rosa! and played the major role in management <u>Rosa</u> Van Beneden-DeKeyser—also played a starring role. In 1944, as a girl of 17, she witnessed the crash. She made a record of the airmen's names which she kept as well as Dewar's photo. she kept them for 62 years

In seeking Dewar's family, Dirk approached the MacLeod Society of Nova Scotia, whose manager, Don MacLeod, on his own initiative, drew up a "Lost and Found" notice for the local newspaper.

Even though I was now living in California, word did reach me by way of my cousin, Mollie Cameron who spotted the notice and called me.

So by one means or another, Dirk tracked down the fliers' next of kin and recruited us. Our chief value lay in the fact that many agencies give information only to next-of—Kin. Colin and I were willing conscripts and we simply followed Dirk's suggestions.

Finally, I have to tell you that we've lost our ladies. Rosa passed away 9 December 2008 at the age of 81 and Mollie passed away early this year, 2012, a few months after her 100th birthday.